THE COVERED BRIDGE

WEST HILL BRIDGE, MONTGOMERY

THE
Covered Bridge

An Old American Landmark

WHOSE ROMANCE, STABILITY, AND CRAFTSMANSHIP
ARE TYPIFIED BY THE STRUCTURES REMAINING
IN VERMONT

By Herbert Wheaton Congdon
Illustrated by Edmund Homer Royce

VERMONT BOOKS

Middlebury

1979

ISBN 0-911570-05-5

© Copyright 1941 by Herbert Wheaton Congdon

First Edition, Stephen Daye Press, 1941
Second Edition, Alfred A. Knopf, 1946
Third Edition, Vermont Books, 1959
Fourth Edition, Vermont Books, 1970
  Reprinted 1970
  Reprinted 1973
  Reprinted 1975
Fifth Edition, Vermont Books, 1979
  Reprinted 1983

CONTENTS

LIST OF ILLUSTRATIONS, *arranged by counties*   7

ACKNOWLEDGMENTS   11

THE COVERED BRIDGE. *A poem.* Anderson M. Scruggs   13

I   FACT AND FANCY—*The importance of environment—Fishermen and swimming boys—"Kissing Bridges"—Some statistics—Investment value.*   15

II   AROUND THE CRACKER BARREL—*The first bridge across the Connecticut—Tucker and his toll bridge—Which is Vermont's oldest bridge?—The bridge that went sailing—Vermont's youngest bridge—Murder and robbery.*   25

III   BY GUESS AND BY GOSH—*Engineers by birth, not education—Why bridges are covered—Wind damage and its prevention—Fooling the experts—Methods of strengthening bridges and their supports—How the bridges were built—Some famous Vermont bridge-builders—The Floating Bridge at Brookfield.*   63

IV   PAYING THE PIPER—*How they raised funds in old days—Lotteries—Toll bridges—Toll-gate keepers versus toll dodgers—Restoration as an economy—Covered wooden railroad bridges.*   91

V   CALLING THE TUNE—*How they knew that a bridge was strong enough—Trusses: what they are—Types of trusses with diagrams and photographs—Bridge portals—Saving the old covered wooden bridges.*   109

REFERENCES   145

INDEX   147

Fig. 1: NORTH BRANCH LAMOILLE RIVER, BELVIDERE

ILLUSTRATIONS

ADDISON COUNTY

		Page
Cornwall-Salisbury; Otter Creek	Fig. 46	69
Ferrisburg; Otter Creek	58	84
Ferrisburg, North; Lewis Creek	52	76
Middlebury; Halpin Bridge, Muddy Branch	21	41
Pulpmill Bridge, Exterior	11	29
Pulpmill Bridge, Interior	12	30
Three-mile Bridge, Exterior	50	74
Three-mile Bridge, Interior	51	75
Salisbury-Cornwall; Otter Creek	46	69
Weybridge-Middlebury;		
Pulpmill Bridge, Exterior	11	29
Pulpmill Bridge, Interior	12	30

BENNINGTON COUNTY

Arlington, West; Bridge at The Green	44	67
Bennington; Henry Bridge, Exterior	15	34
Henry Bridge, Interior	16	35
Sunderland, Chiselville Bridge	20	40

CALEDONIA COUNTY

Barnet; Village Bridge, Stephens River	90	130
Village Bridge, side view	91	131
Danville; Greenbank Hollow Bridge	43	66
Hardwick; Railroad Bridge	69	105
Lyndon; Schoolhouse Bridge	96	136
Road, Lyndonville to Kirby	74	113

CHITTENDEN COUNTY

Charlotte; Lake-shore Bridge, Exterior	25	45
Lake-shore Bridge, Interior	38	60
Charlotte, East; Upper Bridge, Lewis Creek	55	79
Essex; Hubbell's Falls, former bridge	79	117
Westford; Brown's River Bridge	102	142

ESSEX COUNTY

		Page
Guildhall; Bridge to Lancaster	Fig. 61	93
Lemington; Columbia Bridge	63	95
Lunenburg; Mt. Orne Bridge to Lancaster	62	94

FRANKLIN COUNTY

Enosburg; Hopkins Bridge	6	19
Shingle Mill Bridge, Exterior	57	81
Shingle Mill Bridge, Interior	84	123
Fairfax; Lower Bridge, Brown's River	9	23
Village Bridge, Exterior	86	125
Village Bridge, Interior	100	140
Georgia Plains; Pierce's Mill	41	62
Highgate Falls; Former Toll Bridge	3	16
Montgomery; Comstock Bridge in village	56	80
Fuller Bridge in village	5	18
Hectorville Bridge	2	14
Levis Bridge, West Hill Brook	98	138
Longey Bridge	48	71
West Hill Bridge	Frontispiece and 22	42
St. Albans; Creek Bridge, St. Albans Bay	34	56
Swanton; Railroad Bridge	70	106

LAMOILLE COUNTY

Belvidere; North Branch, Lamoille River	1	6
Cambridge; Safford Bridge, Pleasant Valley	80	118
Safford Bridge, side view	81	119
Village Bridge, advertisements	40	61
Village Bridge, Exterior	77	115
Village Bridge, Interior	78	116
Hyde Park; Garfield Bridge, Green River	23	43
Stowe; Miller Brook	75	114
Village Bridge	97	137
Wolcott; Lamoille River	73	112

ORANGE COUNTY

Brookfield; The Floating Bridge	60	89
Newbury; Bedell's Bridge, Connecticut River	64	96
Post Mills; Bridge near village	54	78
Randolph; Bridge between South and East Randolph	19	39
Thetford; Post Mills Bridge	54	78
Tunbridge; First Branch White River	4	17

ORLEANS COUNTY

		Page
Albany; Black River Bridge	Fig. 28	49
Charleston, East; Twin Bridges	36	58
Irasburg; Lord's Creek Bridge	93	133
Upper Bridge, Black River	26	46
Warning sign	39	61
Morgan; Highest Bridge above the Sea	24	44
Troy, North; Lower Bridge, Missisquoi River	47	70
Westfield; Taft Brook Bridge	85	124

RUTLAND COUNTY

Brandon; Private Bridge	67	102
Second Bridge, Otter Creek	99	139
Florence; Hammond Bridge, Otter Creek	17	36
Pittsford; Gorham Bridge, Otter Creek	7	20
Hammond Bridge, Otter Creek	17	36
Proctor-Pittsford; Gorham Bridge	7	20
Proctor; Mead Bridge, Exterior	87	126
Mead Bridge, Interior	88	127
Rutland; Billings Bridge, Otter Creek	27	48
"Old Seventy-six," East Creek	68	103
Twin Bridges, East Creek	35	57

WASHINGTON COUNTY

East Montpelier; Bridge over Winooski	71	108
Marshfield; Private Bridge, Winooski River	66	101
Northfield; Moseley Bridge, Rocky Brook	18	38
Northfield Falls; Village Bridge	94	134
Waitsfield; High Bridge, Clay Brook, winter	101	141
Pine Brook Bridge, Kingpost Truss	72	111
Village Bridge, former appearance	13	31
Village Bridge, present appearance	14	32

WINDHAM COUNTY

Bellows Falls, Tucker Toll Bridge	10	26
Brattleboro, Creamery Bridge	31	53
Dover, West; Open Bridge	42	65
Dummerston, West; West River Bridge	59	88
Guilford; Green River Bridge, Exterior	32	54
Green River Bridge, Interior	33	55

		Page
Newfane; Village Bridge	53	77
Rockingham;		
Bellows Falls; Tucker Toll Bridge	10	26
Saxton's River, Village Bridge	49	72
Townshend; Holland Bridge, West River	29	51
Westminster; Lewis Bridge, Cobb Brook	30	52

WINDSOR COUNTY

Hartland; Martin's Mill Bridge, Lull's Brook	45	68
Royalton; Broad Brook Bridge	83	121
Royalton, South; Abandoned Bridge	8	21
Weathersfield; Upper Bridge, North Branch	82	120
Downer's; Black River Bridge	95	135
West Windsor; Mill Brook Bridge	37	59
Windsor; Windsor-Cornish Toll Bridge	65	98
Woodstock; Taftsville Bridge	89	129

TYPES OF TRUSSES

Burr Truss; Diagram	76	115
Photograph, detail	78	116
Unusual use of Lattice Truss	88	127
Howe Truss; Diagram	92	132
Kingpost Truss	72	111
Lattice or Town Truss	84	123
Treenails in Lattice Truss	58	84
Long Truss	90	130
Mongrel Long Truss	89	129
Old Type Truss, nameless	82	120
Queenpost Truss	73	112
Tied Arch Truss	38	60
Warren Truss	75	114

ACKNOWLEDGMENTS

THIS book could not have been completed without the help of many persons to whom we want to express our gratitude. Richard S. Allen generously put at our disposal a large quantity of material on covered bridges that he has been collecting and arranging for years. Miss Florence Cragin Allen of the Sheldon Museum, Middlebury, has given freely of her time in research. Many important historical items have been furnished by the Government's Historical Records Survey through the generous cooperation of its state supervisor, Henry Howard Eddy. The daily newspapers, the magazines *Yankee* and *Vermonter* and the radio broadcasting privileges of the National Life Insurance Company have given invaluable assistance in getting our appeals for information before a wide audience which responded splendidly.

Town Clerks have searched their records for us in Belvidere, Brookfield, Chelsea, Clarendon, Cornwall, Enosburg, Guildhall, Hartland, Irasburg, Jay, Lemington, Lunenburg, Lyndon, Montgomery, Morgan, Proctor, Rutland (City), Springfield, Stowe, Sudbury, Sunderland, Wallingford, Warren and Worcester. Many individuals have sent in anecdotes, data and suggestions which have been more helpful than they may have realized. Among these are the following:—

Mary R. Allen of the library in Pittsford, Inella C. Bates, May Lamberton Becker of the New York *Herald Tribune,* Alice B. Brainerd, Edith K. Dunton of the Rutland *Herald,* Mary W. Ellis, Mrs. H. B. Farmer, Elizabeth K. Fuller, Mrs. Frank Gates, Annah P. Hazen, Jeannette G. Holbrook, Mrs. L. R. Jones, Mrs. Nelson K. Lewis, Mary Greene Nye of the office of the Vermont Secretary of State, Martha Parsons of the Historical Records Survey, Mrs. Oscar H. Rixford, Mary Gilbert Smith, and Iva M. Young of the Rockingham Public Library at Bellows Falls. Also:—

Nelson Bailey, Stephen Belaski, Professor Thomas E. Boyce, John Branch Sr., Willis N. Cady, G. Stewart Campbell of New Hampshire's Public Works Division, Guy M. Catlin, Professor LeRoy W. Clark of Rensselaer Polytechnic Institute, John Clement, Abner W. Coleman of our state Highway Department, Charles E. Crane, Professor Jasper O. Draffin of the University of Illinois, H. F. Earle of the St. Johnsbury & Lake Champlain railroad, Clayton J. Fuller, Wallace H. Gilpin, Charlie L. Greer, Talbot Hamlin of the Avery Library, Columbia University, B. H. Jewett, Walter E. Jones, M. L. Joslin, Charles T. Middlebrook, C. E., Judge John Morse, Victor Morse, Frederick W. Mould, Hall Park McCullough, John Ormiston, Byron S. Powers, Gratz Powers, Oscar A. Rixford, H. E. Sargent of the state Highway Department, H. L. Scott of the state Planning Board, John Spargo and Edward A. Hoyt of the Vermont Historical Society, Owen R. Washburn, Fred M. Willey, Sydney Wilmot in charge of the publications of the American Society of Civil Engineers, and F. M. Wright.

Our especial thanks are extended to Professor Louis B. Puffer, C.E., of the University of Vermont, for valuable information, advice, and the editing of the technical parts of the book.

HERBERT WHEATON CONGDON
Arlington, Vermont

EDMUND HOMER ROYCE
St. Albans, Vermont

THE COVERED BRIDGE

*Some part of life becomes oblivion;
Something with roots deep buried in the heart
Of simple folk is lost, as one by one,
These pioneers of other days depart.
Only the country folk, whose careless tread
Endears a dusty road, can ever know
The peaceful, clattering joy of rude planks spread
Above a drowsy creek that gleams below.*

*Here was a refuge from the sudden showers
That swept like moving music field and wood,
And here cool, tunnelled dark when sultry hours
Danced with white feet beyond the bridge's hood. . . .
Yet there are soulless men whose hand and brain
Tear down what time will never give again.*

Anderson M. Scruggs

From *Glory of Earth,* by permission of Oglethorpe University, the *New York Times* and the author.

Fig. 2: HECTORVILLE BRIDGE, MONTGOMERY

I

FACT AND FANCY

VERMONT's attractiveness to visitor and native alike depends on something more than the visual charm of mountains and forests. Links that bind us to an earlier, simpler way of life are quite as effective. The old covered bridge, whether it spans a mountain brook or a quiet stream winding through level meadows, carries our thoughts back to the land of half-forgotten dreams. We may grant that few covered bridges possess intrinsic beauty. Honest, straightforward, functional structures, their charm is largely dependent on their surroundings. If you strip them of their usual appurtenances and set them, stark naked, between treeless river banks, perhaps they seem to have been built by the mile and sold by the yard. Little charm would be left to many of the bridges without a background of mountains, trees and rugged boulders.

A more thoughtful study of the bridges themselves shows that this is not always true. It is said that the Chinese think all white folks look alike. They do not discriminate between our homeliness or pulchritude; nor do we, looking at the Chinese. So, a real acquaintance with bridges is a prerequisite to appreciation of their varying degrees of beauty. One purpose of this book is to increase the number of persons who know something about covered bridges and enjoy them more for that knowledge.

The plainest bridge may be a welcome feature in a landscape, and its very plainness emphasize its beauty of proportion. An old toll bridge, long since demolished, stood at Highgate Falls (fig. 3). Severely simple but well proportioned, it was an essential part of a romantic landscape. The picture would be bald and incomplete without it and lacking in attraction if it were a spidery affair of steelwork.

From an old photograph by Truax

Fig. 3: FORMER TOLL BRIDGE, HIGHGATE FALLS

Covered bridges appeal to a more widely varied group of people than almost any other structure. The trout fisherman cherishes the long still pool under the old bridge (fig. 4), a pool with exciting little riffles at head and foot that invite the well cast fly as the deep dark water does the humble worm. Here the city man in waders, his slender split-bamboo and costly equipment serving his skill, vies with the farmer's lad who takes a well-earned rest as his bait dangles from his pole propped on a forked stick stuck in the mud. Small boys know this same place as a sheltered swimming hole where they may splash away without the cramping formality of bathing suits, quite out of sight of the occasional traffic that rumbles overhead. The bird-lover knows that robins, phoebes and some-

Fig. 4: BRIDGE ACROSS FIRST BRANCH, WHITE RIVER, TUNBRIDGE
"*The trout fisherman cherishes the long still pool*"

times swallows, nest among the weathered bridge-timbers, and looks for warblers in the brush along the banks. Bobolinks sing in the long sunny mornings, their rapturous notes accompanied by the sound of the water. Lovers of unspoiled countryside enjoy the sturdy timbers protected by grey, mossy boards half hidden by the sheltering trees whose leaves cast flickering shadows all summer long (fig. 5). Winter reveals the bridge in new guise, its grey bulk prominent against the whiteness of the snow, a tracery of frost-rimed twigs etched like lace against it, the water ice-

Fig. 5: FULLER BRIDGE, BLACK FALL BROOK, MONTGOMERY VILLAGE
"*The sheltering trees cast flickering shadows*"

bound in part and in part diamond clear over anchor-ice instead of the summer pebbles (fig. 6).

Various fanciful names have been applied to covered bridges; the most popular seems to be "kissing bridge" and in the horse-and-buggy days it was a bashful swain indeed, who failed to take advantage of the custom. Today the lover and his lass use a sleek roadster, but they always respect the speed-law "Horses at a walk" or its equivalent. From Marshfield

Fig. 6: HOPKINS BRIDGE, BETWEEN EAST BERKSHIRE AND MONTGOMERY
"Winter reveals the bridge in new guise"

comes a family legend. Grandpa was a shy and lanky boy who had never been able to get to the "poppin' point" with the village belle Hitty, until they were caught by a sudden shower in the old bridge. The rain roared on the roof, assuring privacy as well as giving him courage by its very noise, and finally in a lull of the downpour he managed to stammer "Marry, will you hitty me?", a question that she was fortunately ready and willing to understand. Unfortunately for him, small brother had taken refuge from the same shower and was snugly ensconced among the roof-timbers over their heads. Even the most loyal of small brothers could not keep secret a story like that!

Fig. 7: GORHAM BRIDGE, OTTER CREEK, PITTSFORD-PROCTOR
A "Kissing Bridge" in horse-and-buggy days

Richard S. Allen of Round Lake, New York, has been collecting material on covered wooden bridges for several years and has compiled a census of them covering the entire country. Of course the figures change so fast with highway improvement that absolute accuracy is impossible; nevertheless it is an interesting guide. We learn from it that Vermont has more covered bridges still in use than all the rest of the New England states put together, even if New Hampshire gets credit for half of those

Fig. 8: ABANDONED BRIDGE ACROSS FIRST BRANCH, SOUTH ROYALTON
The town snow-plow lurks here like a dragon in its den

that cross the Connecticut river to us. Perhaps that is to be expected. The surprising thing is that Vermont is in *fourth* place among the rest of the states. Ohio takes the lead with 592 and new ones are still being built almost as fast as the old are taken down. Pennsylvania comes next with 336 and Indiana has 194 still carrying their traffic. In Vermont a census made by the state Highway Department gives about 170 in use, this figure including a few that are of private ownership and counting the Connecticut river bridges as one-half each. There are a few that are abandoned for traffic but have been retained for storage of town road equipment. One of these is the former bridge over First Branch near South Royalton (fig. 8) which has been replaced by a modern bridge near it and the road changed to make safer approaches.

Mr. Allen's census reminds us that covered wooden bridges are by no means an American invention. They are found in all well-forested countries from Norway to China. Some of them are very old. The Kapell Brücke over the Reuss in Luzern, Switzerland, is said to have been built in 1333 but despite the use of tar as preservative for the pine timbers, most of them must have been replaced during the long years. There is a bridge over the Rhine at Stein-Säckingen built in 1685 and as recently as 1924 one was built over the Neckar at Thalhausen in Germany.

In many parts of our country old covered bridges, removed during the course of highway improvement, are being preserved as huge museumpieces. Henry Ford's collection of them is well known; others are being set up in state parks, usually to carry traffic of the weight for which they are adapted. When the Indiana State Highway Commission found it necessary to remove the old Ramp Creek bridge, built in 1837, it was rebuilt in the state park of Brown county. Its removal was due to the change of the highway to a four-lane concrete one, but in the park it is suited to the traffic conditions. It was found to be in almost perfect condition with the exception of a few rotted floor beams and some sub-flooring. Originally of black walnut, the replacements were made of oak.

The value of covered bridges as good long-term investments is being studied by several states; Vermont might well do likewise. If there is a large amount of traffic and if it includes heavy loads of course the covered wooden bridge is outmoded. In localities close to railroads where steel and concrete can be brought to the job cheaply, the cost is usually lower than wood. It is interesting, however, that California finds in remote country districts where transportation of steel and cement is difficult and costly, if there is an ample supply of cheap timber the old fashioned bridge is worth while. It is a mistaken idea that building them is a lost

Fig. 9: LOWER BRIDGE, BROWN'S RIVER, FAIRFAX
Mount Mansfield in the distance

art. The opposite is true. Modern engineering knowledge and practise use several different details such as steel tubing in place of oak pins. If the novelty of steel and concrete can be discounted there are many places where the old style bridge is the wisest investment for the taxpayer, that forgotten and much-abused man. They are already being built for the attraction of tourists in our eastern states.

Even the best modern bridges are not proof against the tremendous power of floods. When they go, destruction is complete and there is little salvage. The buoyancy and homogeneity of the old wooden ones makes them amazingly resistant to complete destruction. After the flood of 1927 a number were rebuilt in new locations to which they had been washed, or even set up in their entirety. In a few cases where the big side frames had been floated away one or two of the long floor timbers (stringers) stayed in place and afforded precarious transit in the emergency.

The timbers of old covered bridges are always in demand. There is a tale that a great match-company paid a round price for the seasoned pine frame of a large bridge that was to be replaced by a wider modern one, only to find that age and vibration had so hardened the wood that it was useless to them. Bridge timbers usually go into barns, but when Bennington built the iron bridge in North Street shortly after the Civil War, the Selectmen sold the old covered bridge to a man who moved it down street and made most of it into a shop. It has served the public since as lunch-room, dressmaker's shop, tin-shop, speakeasy . . . but "mostly barber shop" which it is today, sounder than most of its neighbors and at least as good looking.

All parts of Vermont have their traditions of good men who met calamity with tenacity and courage. Wherever there have been covered bridges there are stories so much alike they are almost folk-tales. One of these usually goes that there had been prolonged rain which had raised the streams dangerously. Toward night the rain turned to wet, blinding snow, driven by the gale. A boy had been sent for the doctor in a case of grave illness. His kindly wife tucked the tired lad in bed while Old Doc started out on horseback into the shrieking, dripping darkness. Reaching the sick man's house, a worried neighbor greeted him. "We'd about given you up, Doc. How on earth did you get here? The bridge went out half an hour after Sammie left."

"Well," said the doctor, "I did have some trouble getting the old mare by one place. It was as dark as the inside of a cat's pocket; I couldn't see a thing for the snow and didn't know where we were. When she balked I gave her a touch of the switch and let her pick her way. She must have footed it over on a stringer."

II

AROUND THE CRACKER BARREL

THE New England town meeting would probably be a less effective organ of democracy without its training-ground, the gathering around the cracker barrel in the general store. Here the elder statesmen hold forth, mingling weighty facts with anecdotes. The disciples, not content with listening, are "reminded" of events that might be true but in any event bear on the matter under discussion. One of the oldest of these tales, already fading into the dimness of history as covered bridges give way to modern improvements, is about a farmer who drove up to a long, dark bridge with an enormous load of hay on his way to market. He sized up the portal with an appraising eye, then looked down the black tunnel to the far end. "I can git through this end all right" said he, "but there ain't room to squeeze through that little hole over thar." So he turned his oxen and plodded home, his hay unsold.

Gathering historical facts about covered bridges has been a similar experience. The foreground material, dealing with recent years, is plentiful and accurate, but search through the dusky years has often resulted in failure. Records are not always specific; for instance, which is "the bridge at the falls" where there are cascades at each end of the village? Occasionally there are gaps in town records because fire has destroyed the books in which the desired information might have been found.

Fortunately, Colonel Hale's bridge at Bellows Falls had such unusual news value that even the conservative journalists of 1785 made much mention of it. It was the very first bridge to span the Connecticut river anywhere in its entire length; it was also a structure of great engineering interest. Like all our connecting bridges with New Hampshire, most of

From an old photograph, courtesy Rockingham Library.

Fig. 10: TUCKER TOLL BRIDGE, BELLOWS FALLS, 1840-1930

it was in that state and it was begun under a grant and charter of its legislature. Enoch Hale, born in Rowley, Massachusetts in 1735, settled at Rindge, New Hampshire about 1760 where he became prominent in that little community. On receiving the charter for his toll bridge he moved a few miles nearer the river and took up his residence in Walpole, opposite Bellows Falls, where his notable bridge was finished in 1785, only two years after the close of the Revolution.

He chose that narrow place in the river where a rock-reef rises from the turbulent waters of the falls, placing his middle pier on its firm foundation. Even with such aid, the two spans were so long that his project was deemed a foolhardy experiment. On its completion, nevertheless, it was rightly hailed as an engineering triumph. It was also of great importance commercially, for it opened the Vermont region to the trade of Boston and the other coastal cities. According to the newspapers of the time the total length was 365 feet, the floor being 50 feet above the water. A well known artist of the period, Frederick J. Blake, made a painting of it which now hangs in the Rockingham Public Library in Bellows Falls. It shows an open bridge such as we build in steel today, with protecting side railings. As described by the papers it was built with four great "stringers" or horizontal timbers, braced from the shore abutments and the middle pier giving an arch-like effect. These stringers were too long to be made in one piece; they had to be spliced, the first example in America of a method of construction which was to become commonplace.

In 1912 the Deutsches Museum of Munich sent a committee to the United States to gather material for the historical engineering exhibits of that famous institution. The American Society of Mechanical Engineers, in its advisory capacity, recommended eight or nine important bridges of which one was Hale's. The Blake painting was copied and is now a part of the museum's collection. Competent authority has stated that without doubt the successful building and use of this structure inspired the erection of others in various parts of the country during the ensuing ten or fifteen years.

Hale got into financial difficulties and mortgaged the bridge to a Mr. Geyer of Boston, who had been trying to buy it for several years as a well-paying investment. The mortgage falling due, Hale borrowed enough from his friends to liquidate it and sent the money to Boston by his son. Unfortunately, this man dallied on the way and arrived too late. Geyer had taken over the property and under the harsh laws of those days, the bridge was his and he held it until his death. His son-in-law Nathaniel Tucker acquired it by his wife's inheritance between 1820 and 1826. His name has been associated with it ever since. A thrifty man, he took excellent care of his chief means of livelihood, but by 1840 it began to show signs of weakness. He called in consultation Sanford Granger, a local bridge builder of high reputation, who recommended that it be taken down as unsafe for the increased traffic load. Tucker engaged him to do this and erect the new structure. This was to be a covered bridge fifteen feet higher above the water, with lattice trusses of the type still seen in many of our bridges. The new Tucker toll bridge stood until 1930, safely carrying an ever-increasing load. In that year it was discovered that an out-of-sight wall block had decayed and irreparable damage had been done to one of the huge trusses, so the old bridge was replaced by the present one.

Except for brief interruptions for repairs, tolls were collected here from 1785 to 1905 when it was made free. Mr. Tucker, a picturesque and fiery little man, collected them personally almost to the day of his death. An ardent Episcopalian, he advertised every year during his regime to the effect that "all those from New Hampshire points who wish to attend Christmas service at Immanuel church" could pass the bridge free of tolls. He was less lenient to those who disobeyed the notice at the portals "Walk your Horses." There was keen rivalry between drivers of the competing coach lines. One of them, anxious for a record, made this last lap of his journey at a rattling gallop. Irate Mr. Tucker followed him to the hotel shouting "You run my bridge! You run my bridge! The fine is TWO DOLLARS!" Triumphant driver Brooks, his eyes sparkling, drew out his wallet to pay. Tucker, his temper as quick to fade as to rise, turned away muttering "Well, don't you ever do it again."

It would be interesting to know which of Vermont's bridges is the oldest. The problem is unsolved, so far, even after much searching for accurate dates. The evidence points to the Pulpmill bridge (fig. 11) as at least fifteen years older than any of which there are authentic records. First known as "the bridge near the paper mill" on the outskirts of Middlebury village, the name of Papermill bridge followed naturally and lasted until the old mill was reopened to make paper-pulp, when the present name came into use. There is only one other double-lane bridge

Fig. 11: PULPMILL BRIDGE, OTTER CREEK, MIDDLEBURY-WEYBRIDGE
Is this Vermont's oldest bridge still in use?

left in Vermont, and probably not over six or seven remain elsewhere. In the early days it was owned and operated as a toll bridge by the Waltham Turnpike Company which was dissolved in 1828. After that date its maintenance was shared by the towns of Middlebury and Weybridge, the boundary line being the middle of Otter Creek which the bridge spans. Neither town has any record of building a new bridge at this site. It is true that some of their books are missing, having been destroyed by fire, and the turnpike company's books are lost.

There is, however, an act of the state legislature that may have a bearing on the problem. It was passed in 1808, granting certain privileges to the turnpike company. It mentions their "bridge by the paper-mill on

Fig. 12: PULPMILL BRIDGE, MIDDLEBURY-WEYBRIDGE
Showing the reinforcing laminated arches

Otter Creek, which bridge has been lately erected and may stand a number of years. . . ." It goes on to direct that the company may erect its tollgate when they "shall have covered and put a railing on said bridge" and closes with the proviso that "a bridge shall be erected . . . within twelve years from the passing of this act." The construction of the trusses of the present bridge suggests that it may date back to the period 1808-1820.

This construction is known as the "Burr-arch" truss and is well shown

Photo by Walter E. Jones.

Fig. 13: WAITSFIELD VILLAGE BRIDGE AS IT USED TO BE

in the accompanying illustration (fig. 12) together with the reinforcing arch known to have been placed in 1859 or 1860. The Burr truss was first used in 1804 at Waterford, New York, and was patented in 1817. It has vertical posts and sloping braces with an arch of segments of hewn timber bolted to the frame. About 1860 the Pulpmill bridge needed strengthening and Deacon David E. Boyce added the "laminated arches" composed of ten layers of planks bent around the old arches as patterns and securely fastened to one another and the frame. In that same year he added similar arches to the Three-mile bridge farther up the creek (fig. 50). This is known to have been built in 1836. It is framed with the lattice type of truss which was first used about ten years earlier and rapidly supplanted the Burr truss in popular favor. All the other bridges in these two towns are framed with lattice type of truss and were mostly built by the Boyce family. The fact that Burr trusses were used in the Pulpmill bridge sug-

Fig. 14: WAITSFIELD VILLAGE BRIDGE AS IT IS TODAY

gests it was built by outsiders, which points to the Waltham Turnpike company as the employers, a company chiefly owned in Vergennes. So, with circumstantial evidence only, the defense rests.

If the Pulpmill bridge is not our oldest, the crown of seniority is not easy to award. There were very destructive floods in 1830, 1832 and again in 1839 which seem to have wrought widespread havoc. Any bridge still in use and known to have been built before 1839 is at least one of Vermont's oldest.

The village bridge in Waitsfield (fig. 13) is known to have been completed in 1833, replacing one destroyed by the 1830 flood. It spans Mad river at the Big Eddy, one end securely resting on a great ledge. Built of well-seasoned spruce, it stands today much as it was built except for improvements like the "wart of a sidewalk" (fig. 14) and holes cut in the boarding of the sides to admit the daylight thought necessary by moderns. For well over a century it has carried its leisurely traffic and has been the favored clubhouse and playground of many generations of small boys, especially on rainy days.

The Henry bridge across the Walloomsac in Bennington town (fig. 15) is of less certain date, possibly soon after 1832 when a freshet carried away bridges and dams on the tributary Paran creek a short distance upstream. It certainly is not the same bridge, as local legends would have us believe, where embattled Vermont farmers bluffed a New York sheriff and his posse on July 19th, 1771, although it is at the same site on the old highway between Bennington and Albany, New York. James Breckinridge had settled a farm nearby under grant from the royal governor of New Hampshire. The same land had been granted to another settler by the governor of the province of New York under the assumption that his colony owned the land all the way to the Connecticut river. The disgruntled New York settler, finding his land occupied by another, applied to Sheriff Ten Eyck of Albany to protect his rights. One fine summer day the sheriff set out at the head of a force of about three hundred men to evict the trespasser Breckinridge. His neighbors had learned via grapevine telegraph of the threatened attack and rallied to his protection. Half a dozen men held the Henry bridge (not a covered one then) and other detachments, their weapons plainly visible, were posted on the high ground beyond when the *posse comitatus* came in sight.

The Yorkers halted. The sheriff demanded a parley and was conducted to the Breckinridge cabin which he found occupied by "eighteen determined men" behind loop-holed barricades. These Vermonters declared their loyalty to the King but also their determination to defend their rights. The sheriff, in a serious predicament, returned to his men and ordered them to advance. The sight of those lean, grim Vermonters si-

Photo by Herbert Wheaton Congdon.

Fig. 15: HENRY BRIDGE, WALLOOMSAC RIVER, BENNINGTON

lently watching, blunted the effects of his harangue. The posse marched back to Albany.

The present Henry bridge enters history with Albany again playing an important part, but this time as a much-appreciated market for the output of the iron mines of Bennington and vicinity. As it was originally constructed, it was of the familiar lattice design, quite able to carry the usual farm traffic but by no means strong enough for the heavy loads of pig-iron, creaking ponderously along on huge wagons each drawn by several yokes of oxen. Not long after it was built, and probably well before 1845, it was strengthened by the simple expedient of building a second

Fig. 16: INTERIOR OF HENRY BRIDGE, BENNINGTON
The doubled trusses make it Vermont's strongest bridge

Fig. 17: HAMMOND BRIDGE, OTTER CREEK, PITTSFORD
A bridge that went on a voyage

set of lattices into the trusses (fig. 16), making it the strongest bridge of its time and size in the state although the exterior shows a lamentable tendency to lean to one side, probably due to lack of proper lateral bracing. The heavy loads of iron are in a distant past; the bridge serves its present traffic admirably, now that the main highway is a concrete one high on the hills to the south. During the flood of 1927 when the fine modern bridges had gone out, this century-old bridge was a godsend, maintaining traffic when communications were sorely needed.

During that same flood the Hammond bridge in **Pittsford** (fig. 17), lacking any wartime history, did its own adventuring. Otter Creek winds sluggishly through level fields for many miles. In such a terrain there is no chance for flood waters to run off so the stream rose higher and higher, spreading far out into the meadows. At last the old bridge felt "the thrill of life along her keel" and was floated off the abutments, a clumsy ark. When Asa Nourse built it in 1843 he gave no thought to plimsoll-marks or stream-lining. He just built a good solid bridge, and at that he was content to be paid in notes when cash ran out. The voyage was a short one, a mere mile and a half, when the bridge caught in the banks. The flood over, the authorities were delighted to find they had not lost a bridge; it was only misplaced. Empty oil barrels were lashed to the structure to buoy it up enough to clear the shoals, now so much nearer the surface, and it was slowly towed upstream and reset on new and higher abutments. There is little traffic on that quiet road; the bridge should serve for many years to come.

The Hammond bridge and its downstream neighbor, the Gorham bridge (fig. 7), were two of many that played a giant game of "going to Jerusalem" in that flood. Some were reset on abutments far from where they started while others were taken apart and rebuilt; those too completely wrecked for restoration were used as sources of materials for temporary bridges. Much of the rest went into new barns. There was little salvage from the modern bridges which the flood had destroyed. Huge masses of concrete were a dead loss. Twisted steel was often buried under tons of boulders. The old wooden bridges had shown their investment value again. It set some highway engineers to thinking that perhaps they had real value aside from sentiment.

Nevertheless, Vermont's newest wooden bridge is already nearly fifty years old; over Rocky Brook, Northfield (fig. 18). It is an old-fashioned bridge with shapely arched portals, their boarding stripped with narrow vertical battens according to the local custom. The builders were the Moseleys, father and son. There is another charming little bridge be-

Fig. 18: MOSELEY BRIDGE OVER ROCKY BROOK, NORTHFIELD
Vermont's youngest bridge: 1899

tween South and East Randolph (fig. 19) which bears the date "1909" painted in the gables and therefore is supposed to be a new one. It is not, for a little investigation made clear that this was merely the date of restoration. The evidence of the species of truss used confirmed our opinion that it is a very old bridge, originally without roof. Doubtless the trusses were boarded on both sides at first, for protection, as was often done in the case of little bridges (fig. 42).

There was a bad flood in 1869 which took out every bridge and most of the roads in Sunderland. One of these was the bridge close to the sur-

Fig. 19: BETWEEN SOUTH AND EAST RANDOLPH
An old bridge restored in 1909

face of the millpond in the little hamlet called Chiselville. The selectmen, anxious to avoid a repetition of so costly a disaster, decided to change the location when rebuilding. The old approaches had been down steep banks on either side, one of them with a sharp curve. Daniel Oatman was called into conference, and he recommended placing the bridge between the high cliffs which flanked the dam, a location that would call for lofty falsework, but he said, "I'll build you a bridge there that'll never wash out." There it stands 40 feet above the water and 117 feet long, a daring structure and still staunch (fig. 20). Apparently the selectmen were sure of the strength of their bridge, for the almost-obliter-

Photo by Herbert Wheaton Congdon.

Fig. 20: CHISELVILLE BRIDGE, ROARING BRANCH, SUNDERLAND

ated signs over the portals read "One dollar fine for horses faster than a walk" instead of the usual two dollars; or possibly they realized how poor people were. Our highest bridge is the Halpin one in Middlebury (fig. 21), a foot higher than Chiselville's. Montgomery's West Hill bridge (fig. 22), like the Garfield one (fig. 23), looks higher than it is because of the tumbling brook, a succession of waterfalls, but Garfield's can claim high altitude, being more than 1100 feet above sea-level. The altitude record for Vermont, however, is held by a picturesque small bridge in Morgan (fig. 24) which is the top bridge of the state, 1450 feet above tidewater. The gently rolling plateau gives little impression of an altitude record!

Fig. 21: HALPIN BRIDGE, MUDDY BRANCH, MIDDLEBURY
This once served a marble mill

Fig. 22: WEST HILL BRIDGE, MONTGOMERY

Fig. 23: GARFIELD BRIDGE, GREEN RIVER, HYDE PARK

Fig. 24: BRIDGE IN MORGAN, VERMONT'S HIGHEST ABOVE THE SEA

At the other extreme is the very old lake-shore bridge in Charlotte (fig. 25), for Lake Champlain is only about a hundred feet above the ocean.

Years ago the selectmen used to specify that a new bridge was to be "a load of hay wide and high," giving the builder considerable latitude. It always meant a one-way bridge, but not always as generous a passageway as that in the upper bridge in Irasburg (fig. 26). The accepted courtesy of the road gave the right of way to the first team on the bridge, but in the early days of motoring, drivers of the swifter vehicles were less courteous than they are today. The mail-carrier had driven his buggy about half

Fig. 25: ON LAKE CHAMPLAIN'S SHORE, CHARLOTTE

way across when one of the new contraptions clattered on to the other end. Obviously there was not room to pass and the auto came to a reluctant halt in front of the astonished but placid horse. The begoggled driver demanded that the buggy be backed out to let him by.

"If he hadn't been so uppity I'd have done it," Anse said as he told his experience. "He got to cussin', got out and took my horse by the bridle and allowed he'd make me; so I pulled my gun and told him I was carryin' the mail and he'd better shut up and back out himself. He did it, too."

While carrying a road across a river was the chief purpose of a bridge, it served a good many others in old times. George D. Aiken, United States Senator from Vermont, told one of his audiences about a farmer who had been hounded by his wife for months to get a new suit of clothes. One day

Fig. 26: UPPER BRIDGE, BLACK RIVER, IRASBURG

he hitched up to take some eggs and garden-stuff in to the village hotel. He got such a good price for them that he decided to please and surprise his wife by getting that new suit. He found what he wanted, had it put up in a bundle and set it in the back of the buggy. As it was getting on towards sundown he decided his hired man would do the chores and he might as well show up in his new clothes. He stopped the horse in the dusk of a covered bridge and stripped off the ragged old ones. They really didn't seem fit for a scarecrow, so he threw them through the opening in the side of the bridge for the swift current to dispose of. Then he reached over the back of the seat for his bundle. It was gone! It had bobbed out somewhere along the road! He drove home clad only in his shirt. His wife was surprised . . . . but not pleased.

Shelters from hot sun or soaking rain, some old bridges were used for camp-meetings in an emergency, or even as drill floors for the local militia. It was the small boys, though, who discovered their value as recreation centers long years before such luxuries came to the rural regions. One of these boys grew up to write:—"Our bridge was the community house on rainy days; no reading room or piano, but plenty to keep a lively youngster busy. A very decent place it was to run off sprints when bare feet were tough enough to stand the slivery floor, sprints held in spite of those stern signboards that threatened a fine of 'Two dollars for passing this bridge faster than a walk.' The rods and braces overhead served to hand-over-hand and chin until arms gave out and one was deposited with tingling feet on the floor below.

"There were dusty timbers to clamber over and initials to be carved with the stub of a jack-knife always found in a country boy's pocket. Wonderful hidey-holes served for councils of war, and hiding could be safely and swiftly done when occasion demanded. Dingy glass boxes, one at either end, held still dingier kerosene lamps supposed to light the dark cavern of this village bridge at night. It was found that captured bullfrogs placed in them made hurried exits when the door was opened by the unsuspecting boy-janitor who came at dusk to light up."

The Cracker-barrel Club has told many a tale of more sordid events connected with the gloomy shelter of covered bridges. The Billings bridge near Rutland (fig. 27) has a long list of crimes of violence connected with its century of existence. In a lonely spot, it made an excellent lurking place for highwaymen. Avery Billings saved himself from a gang of that sort one cloudy night. On the way home from the village he pulled his saddle-horse down to a walk as he entered the bridge. An unseen hand seized the bridle, but Billings spurred his mount, rode the robbers down and escaped. Another man was less fortunate. On his way to Rutland with a considerable sum of money to buy railroad tickets for a western trip, he was set upon, robbed and murdered. His body was not found

Fig. 27: BILLINGS BRIDGE, OTTER CREEK, RUTLAND
Once a lurking place for highwaymen

for many days; his attackers were never identified. Rutland's "Old '76" bridge was the scene of a particularly unsavory murder in the present century. A rustic Venus inveigled an Italian laborer to its dusky concealment where her accomplice "surprised" them. A fight ensued which ended with the death and robbery of the unfortunate foreigner.

Fortunately, most bridge-stories are less gloomy. One is told of the shapely small bridge in Albany (fig. 28) which crosses Black river at the foot of the steep half-mile Hitchcock hill, the road making a sharp turn. "Wib" Eldridge was a tinsmith by trade. He had acquired his peg-leg from an accident, but nature was responsible for the impediment in his speech. One day Wib started out in his one-horse wagon to get a pig. On the way back, piggie in a basket beside him on the seat, the breeching

Fig. 28: BLACK RIVER BRIDGE, ALBANY

broke as he drove down Hitchcock hill. The horse ran away, completely out of control as the heavy wagon, banging against his hind legs, urged him on. As Wib told it later in the village store, "Says I to myself, says I, I'll never make that turn in Trist's world." He didn't. The whole outfit went straight ahead into the river. After his friends had pulled man, horse and pig out of the water with no serious damage to any of them, Wib piped up "By funder, gimme my pig; I'm goin' home."

Vermont has some haunted bridges; usually the spirits are of the bottled variety, but there are others. The Brattleboro *Reformer* laid one ghost. Many years ago Seth Allen was hired to reshingle the roof of the Scott bridge in Townshend. This is a very long three-span bridge, one being over West river, the others crossing a deep gully on dry land. Seth was given to doing things differently from most folks. He decided to do this job by the light of the full moon, using no staging. Unless one happened to stand at one side to see him on the roof, there was no sign of activity. Late on one of these moonlit nights Leslie Lowe was driving home from the village behind his old black horse Jerry. All was silent as he entered the long black tunnel of the bridge. Suddenly, when he was about half way across, a great din of hammering began overhead. Lowe could not imagine what it was; Jerry gave him no time to figure it out. Sure that the devil himself was after him, the old horse started off at top speed. One of the wildest rides ensued that Leslie Lowe ever took. If the hill-road home hadn't winded Jerry, he might have kept running until morning.

Not far from Scott bridge the Holland bridge (fig. 29) crosses West river. It is a fine structure of two spans, wide and long. According to the town records it was built in 1875 at a cost of $4,094.04, a small sum for so large a bridge. In 1935, while it was undergoing routine repairs, jacks were placed under it near the middle pier in an attempt to remove the slight sag there. When they began to take hold it was found that the old trusses were so firmly compacted by years of use that the shore end was lifted several inches from its bearing. Satisfied that the bridge needed no straightening, the repair gang let it down again. Their chief "improvement" was to paint the new side boarding green, the only bridge of that color in the state.

There have been several bridges on this site. One of the most interesting traditions is of an attempt to build an *iron* bridge at a point a little south of the present structure. Word-of-mouth legend relates that the iron was obtained from old cart-wheel tires and similar sources, wrought into bridge-members at a temporary forge set up in the adjoining meadow. When the falsework was removed the bridge collapsed into the river, carrying a man down with it and breaking his leg. Records of town meetings shed interesting side-lights on this story. In 1807 an appropriation was asked to buy "iron oil for paint for the new bridge." The 1808

Fig. 29: HOLLAND BRIDGE, WEST RIVER, TOWNSHEND

meeting refused to indemnify Joshua Hide of Putney for injuries received in falling off the bridge. In 1820 the selectmen were directed to sell the iron from "the old bridge" and the 1822 meeting called on them for an accounting of the sale. What may have been our first iron bridge seems to have been a failure, so perhaps it is kinder to cease research.

Road improvement changes our census of bridges so fast that it is hard to state with accuracy whether Lamoille or Windham county has the greater number of covered wooden bridges still in use. The score is about twenty-two to twenty-three; it may be a tie before this book is published.

Fig. 30: LEWIS BRIDGE, COBB BROOK, WESTMINSTER (1838)

Windham's Lewis bridge in Westminster town (fig. 30) is an old-timer and looks it, with its old-fashioned portal and well-weathered boarding. It was built in 1838 by Erastus M. Holton who was instructed to make it like a neighboring bridge that had been erected by Sanford Granger of Bellows Falls. The 1843 freshet washed out an abutment, but the trusses were not damaged. Granger was called in to make the repairs. He raised it from its former level to the present one and lengthened it twenty-four feet. His work still shows plainly, the new timbers being spliced to the old with the usual wooden pins. A skilled workman, he did a fine job.

Brattleboro, the most populous town in Windham county, has only

Photo by Herbert Wheaton Congdon.

Fig. 31: CREAMERY BRIDGE, WHETSTONE BROOK, BRATTLEBORO

the Creamery bridge (fig. 31) left of the many famous ones of older days. Strange to say, instead of its being tucked away on some quiet country road, it is on the very border of that busy village. It was built in 1879 to replace one swept away by a freshet in Whetstone brook, and is in a longevity contest with an iron one built the same year at Elliot street. The selectmen were rightly proud that when it was contracted for they were able to replace hemlock, included in the bid, with the stronger, lighter

Fig. 32: GREEN RIVER BRIDGE, GUILFORD

spruce and still save $100. It has been well maintained so it will give some light on the relative durability of wood and metal bridges when one of the two has to be taken down.

The neighboring town of Guilford is such a rural one, with no villages of any size, that one would expect to find many old bridges in it. Only one is left, however, over Green river (figs. 32, 33). The many abandoned farms in this town are being bought up for summer homes by people who like the unspoiled simplicity of country life. It is a pity that

Fig. 33: GREEN RIVER BRIDGE, GUILFORD
The town stores its derrick here

when bridges have been wrecked by storm they have not been replaced by the old-fashioned sort, so much more in keeping with the character of the landscape and perfectly capable of carrying the light and infrequent traffic. Given proper designs and supervision by the highway department of the state, even inexperienced carpenters have been found capable

Photo by W. D. Chandler, about 1900.

Fig. 34: FORMER FISHING BRIDGE AT THE CREEK, ST. ALBANS BAY

bridge builders elsewhere. Perhaps what is needed is the spur of public opinion based on the realization of the investment value of a good covered wooden bridge.

The Green river bridge is an attractive one. Its neat trimmed arch suggests that there is someone in authority who cares about this example of the old way of doing. Evidently, when it has undergone repairs, care has been exercised to keep the old appearance as well as to maintain its strength. It seems to have been found useful, too, for the town derrick is stored in the interior, a lengthy piece of apparatus that is going to last longer because of being stored in a dry place. Perhaps it is the same person who has neatly scraped off the advertising posters that still are found in many bridge interiors. Often these advertise stores long closed, their

Fig. 35: TWIN BRIDGES ACROSS EAST CREEK, RUTLAND
The stream takes its choice of channels

proprietors dead and forgotten, and products superseded by those nationally advertised by other means.

Tourists visiting Yellowstone park know the famous fishing bridge there. Few know we once had a fishing bridge in Vermont. The old bridge across a shallow creek entering St. Albans bay (fig. 34) has been gone for many years now, replaced by a modern structure, but fishing stories are still told about it. One of its habitués, a zealous fisherman given to tying his own flies, often of experimental patterns, went early one morning to try out his latest creation. Under the bridge there was a spot hard to get at without being seen by the fish. Luckily, he had noted a place where it could be reached through a broken floor board. He tiptoed to the break, lay down flat on his stomach and cautiously dropped

Fig. 36: TWIN BRIDGES, CLYDE RIVER, EAST CHARLESTON

in his precious fly on a hand-line. At once there was a surge, and he was fast to one of those veritable monsters for which fishermen live. He played it skilfully until it was exhausted and drew it up, hardly able to wiggle its tail. To his dismay, the fish was too big to get through the crevice in the board. The great fish, with a final flop, broke the leader. The fisherman lost fish, fly, and—when he tried to tell the story—the last shreds of his reputation for veracity.

Man is born to trouble; even if he is a selectman. Could anything be more mortifying than to spend the taxpayers' money in replacing a washed-out bridge with a fine new one, only to have the next freshet cut a new channel and leave the bridge across dry land? That happened

Fig. 37: MILL BROOK BRIDGE, WEST WINDSOR

when Nicholas M. Powers built a bridge for Rutland's selectmen over East creek in 1849. The next year he duplicated it over the shifted stream and the Twin bridges (fig. 35) resulted. The accident proved a boon; the two channels have taken care of all later floods.

Up in Orleans county East Charleston has twin bridges, too (fig. 36),

Fig. 38: TIED ARCH, LAKE-SHORE BRIDGE, CHARLOTTE

where the Clyde river meanders through flat, marshy meadows. Unlike Rutland's identical twins, these are of the similar type, alike as to their exteriors but for some unknown reason constructed with different sorts of trusses. Their high steep roofs fit them for the deep snows of the north country. The West Windsor folks built their Mill brook bridge (fig. 37) of an almost identical design. It is many miles south of Charleston and has the same high steep roof, yet it is in a region that is not noted for heavy snow. One wonders at the similarity. The truss used in it is a peculiar one, rare in the state, called a "tied-arch" truss (fig. 38). As the picture shows, it consists of an arch built up of five thicknesses of heavy planks bolted together and to the stout framework of the bridge. Toward the bottom a board is spiked to the posts, but the true tie is out of sight

Fig. 39: OLD WARNING SIGN   Fig. 40: BRIDGE ADVERTISEMENTS

under the floor and consists of the heavy stringer timber that reaches from shore to shore. The illustration is of the Lake-shore bridge in Charlotte, but the arch is the same as in the Mill brook bridge.

The dry wood of an old bridge seems an invitation to destruction by fire. It is odd that so few bridges have been burned. When such a loss occurs it is sure to get newspaper space. One old bridge "went west" literally, as the river runs in that direction. Let the Burlington *Free Press* tell the story:—

"Jeffersonville, July 22, 1929.—Driven to frenzy by pain, two valuable work horses late this afternoon raced from the Curtis meadow to the highway, the hayrack blazing. On the bridge to the Bakersfield road the animals collapsed and died of their burns.

"The structure caught fire and was totally destroyed. What remained of it collapsed and fell into the Lamoille river."

Fig. 41: FORMER PIERCE'S MILL BRIDGE, GEORGIA PLAINS

An odd mixture of trusses

III

BY GUESS AND BY GOSH

THE boarders on a Vermont farm needed a rowboat from which to fish the nearby lake. "I'll make you one," said the farmer. They wanted to know what previous experience in boat-building he had, and when it was revealed that he had none, the question was asked how he planned to go about it. "Oh, I'll work by guess and by gosh" was his characteristic reply, which is a good description of the way in which many of our covered bridges were built.

The civil engineers who are called upon to build today's bridges make their calculations from definite knowledge of the strength and behavior of their materials under given conditions. They have mathematical formulas as well as graphic methods of design with which to do their work. Powerful but sensitive machines in great testing laboratories are used in experiments on full-sized beams to learn how much they will carry. The "factor of safety" or amount of extra strength that must be provided for unpredictable emergencies is a matter of law as well as good practise.

All of this procedure has been developed since the covered-bridge era. It was unknown to old-time builders and only hazily understood by their successors. To be sure, professional engineers have been studying and developing their science for a couple of centuries, but before 1850 bridge-building was an empiric craft, not an exact science. The builders of Vermont's highway bridges were not college-taught professional engineers. They were ingenious and thoughtful men of little schooling, guided by their training under skilled master-craftsmen and educated by their own experience. They worked "by guess and by gosh," and their success was remarkable.

The calibre of these pioneer bridge constructors can be appreciated best by modern engineers. Professor Robert Fletcher, late Director of Dartmouth's Thayer School of Civil Engineering, with Jonathan Parker Snow, a prominent Boston engineer as collaborator, has written an authoritative essay on the development of wooden bridges. In it tribute is paid to our early bridge builders, who had little to guide them in their work except experience and common-sense.

"These men," they state, "were real engineers. The historians of America have generally ignored them, perhaps because they were regarded as mere carpenters. They were among the empire builders. They are more deserving of mention in history and inscriptions on memorial tablets than many who have achieved less for their country. They are comparable to the 'Brothers of the Bridge' who built and maintained the great stone bridges during the Middle Ages." There is good reason, then, for laymen to admire the works of their hands which carry the traffic of our back roads across Vermont's clear streams.

Our pioneering forefathers got along until late in the 1700's with fords for small streams and ferries across the Connecticut river. Even half a century later thrifty taxpayers arose in town meeting to protest against a bridge if there was a good ford near the site. "Taxes are high enough," was their argument. Bridges were bound to come, however. There were progressives far back in ox-team days, long before the horse-and-buggy era. Those first bridges were not covered. They were too close to their prototype, two logs felled across a stream, floored with poles. It was found that the trusses of the supporting framework would last longer if they were boarded in, protected against the weather. The result was the boarded open bridge like that in West Dover (fig. 42), a type that continued in use long after roofed bridges had become universal for wider streams.

Observant bridge builders soon realized that their structures needed protection against the wind. There was a tendency for all trusses to be

Photo by Herbert Wheaton Congdon

Fig. 42: OPEN BRIDGE, WEST DOVER

blown into a leaning position, if not wrecked. As this was a hinge motion from the more solid floor, the cure was obviously to be found in overhead bracing. This framework needed protection from the rain — in other words, a roof. The roof trusses could be used in turn for attaching braces between their timbers and the side frames of the bridge, the diagonal members that show inside most bridges.

And so the covered bridge was born, protected against the weather by boarded sides and shingled roof like the familiar barn. This development took place during the early 1800s and was the topic of lively discussion. Would a longer life for the bridge compensate for the greater cost? Palmer, a famous bridge engineer and builder, had declared as early as

Fig. 43: GREENBANK HOLLOW BRIDGE, DANVILLE

1806, "I am an advocate for weather-boarding and roofing, although there are some who may say it argues much against my interest." By 1810 the case for greater durability had won and the demand for covered bridges was general.

Today's laymen often write queries to the papers, "Why were the old bridges covered?" An early Scottish traveler, writing of his American experiences, comments, "The people of New England have the surprising custom of building woodsheds on top of their bridges." He was apparently willing to let it go at that, without asking "Why?" The correct answer is "For protecting costly framework against decay, thus assuring greater durability, and to stiffen it against gales."

Photo by Herbert Wheaton Congdon.

Fig. 44: BRIDGE AT THE GREEN, WEST ARLINGTON

As people learned through experimenting that a roof was well worth its extra cost, since it stiffened the entire bridge, a number of the open bridges were changed over to covered ones. The Greenbank Hollow bridge in Danville (fig. 43) is one, and there are a good many other converted bridges among these illustrations. As a rule they can be identified by the independence of the comparatively light wall-framing holding up the roof from the more massive trusses that carry the bridge load. The former bridge at Pierce's Mill near Georgia Plains (fig. 41) is rather unusual in that the bridge truss looks rather flimsy while the wall that carries the roof framing is a sturdy X-truss. Perhaps this was the original part, and the A-shaped truss was a later addition intended to strengthen the bridge.

Fig. 45: MARTIN'S MILL BRIDGE, LULL'S BROOK, HARTLAND

It took a good many years before the necessity of strengthening a bridge against damage from gales was fully appreciated. Anybody who has navigated an umbrella in New York's downtown canyons knows what astonishing pressure the wind can exert against a small area. The boarded sides of a bridge act like potent sails for that stationary craft. Wind is apt to follow the line of the stream and may push with tremendous force during "horizontal weather" as the Other Professor called it. A hurricane may do serious damage.

The bridge at the Green in West Arlington (fig. 44), built in 1851, was blown off its abutments and toppled into the Battenkill when it was still the "new bridge." There it lay, held in almost its usual location,

Fig. 46: OTTER CREEK BRIDGE, CORNWALL-SALISBURY
Leaning like Pisa's Tower and as solid

when a Sandgate farmer with business to transact at the Green found his passage a trifle difficult. Nothing daunted, he crossed over on the flat side of the bridge and returned by the same route. The bridge was too heavy to be lifted back by any apparatus available so it was taken apart and rebuilt. This time they tied it to the banks by stout iron rods, defying future storms and floods so successfully that it is still in use. It is the last covered bridge left in town.

It is thought that the best practise is to fasten the anchor rods to the lower corners of the bridge, where they serve to hold the bridge against high water as well as wind. Sometimes they were secured to the upper

Fig. 47: LOWER BRIDGE, MISSISQUOI RIVER, NORTH TROY

corners, as in the bridge near Martin's mill over Lull's brook in Hartland (fig. 45). The Pierce's mill bridge (fig. 41) was anchored with steel wire cable, a more modern material.

Wind can damage a bridge without blowing it away. Trees bent by prevailing winds from one direction are common enough and the bridge over Otter Creek on the boundary between Cornwall and Salisbury (fig. 46) suggests this effect. An observant bridge builder would learn a lesson from this and see to it that his next bridge had ample bracing between the trusses and the roof-framing, which seems to be scanty in this one. Sometimes sloping braces outside the frame were used, a fashion carried over from the open bridges like the Dover one (fig. 42) and shown in a rather exaggerated form in the lower bridge over the Missisquoi river near North Troy (fig. 47). Such braces give an especially solid effect which is

Fig. 48: LONGEY BRIDGE BETWEEN EAST BERKSHIRE AND MONTGOMERY

heightened by the wide spread of the roof. Instead of the customary vertical boarding on the sides, this bridge has clapboards which, when new, must have added to its neat appearance. The trusses of most bridges were boarded on the inside for a short space near the ends as protection from driving storms, a device that is omitted in this case.

This boarded space shows in the Head or Longey bridge between East Berkshire and Montgomery (fig. 48). Such sheltered bits of wall were greatly appreciated by old-time bill posters. More than one small boy has been late to school because he paused too long in rapt contemplation of the glories of the coming circus. Today there are only tattered rem-

Fig. 49: VILLAGE BRIDGE, SAXTON'S RIVER, ROCKINGHAM
A bridge that fooled the engineers

nants of the gaily colored posters, for covered bridges have outlived circuses in country districts. An old lady remembers that during her school days she walked the stringers of this bridge while it was under construction about 1863.

In the early days of motoring it used to be said there were two kinds of chickens: the quick and the dead. There are two kinds of bridges, too; the kind that is able to carry modern traffic far in excess of expectations, and that which fell down in its youth from poor guessing on the part of its builder. The village bridge in Saxton's River (fig. 49) was built in 1870 as a single span bridge. After a few years it was strengthened by adding laminated arches like those in the Pulpmill bridge (fig. 11). More recently the highway engineers decided it needed the support of a stone pier in midstream and spent a lot of money building one. The following spring the pier went out with the ice during a freshet and was never replaced, but the bridge is still taking its punishment.

"When a long strip of cement road was laid through Westminster and Putney on routs 5," says the Brattleboro *Reformer*, "traffic was detoured through the village of Saxton's River and this bridge carried it all for several months. At one end the approach is down a steep hill. Heavy trucks roared down it, hurdled the little bump at the entrance and landed on the floor with a thud. After a while it was discovered that the stringers supporting the floor had been snapped and all that kept the trucks from dropping into the river was a collection of iron rods that had been put underneath the floor as braces some years before." That is a compliment not only to the unknown builder, but also the purity of the iron of which the rods were made. Pure iron will not rust away as steel does. It merely gathers a brown patina.

When a flood came there was plenty of excitement in the neighborhood of a bridge. Its loss would mean more than inconvenience; taxes would have to be raised. The Vermonter is yet to be born who does not think taxes are too high, especially his. Every effort was bent, therefore, on saving the bridge. One way was to remove as many of the side-boards on the upstream side as possible and let the rushing water tear off those on the downstream side. A stoutly-framed bridge, well anchored to the shore, could stand a lot of water above the floorboards without going out unless the abutments were undermined by the swirling current and the bridge wrecked through their failure.

"My father had a deep respect for these old bridges," writes a friend, "and felt it a mistake to replace them with less secure ones. When I was a young girl he was driving me to Hanover one day in the spring when the Connecticut was very high. We saw a crowd of people near the bridge

Fig. 50: THREE-MILE BRIDGE, OTTER CREEK, MIDDLEBURY (1836)

and asked what it was all about. They said they were waiting for the bridge to go out; it had moved two feet already. Father said he wanted to cross the old bridge once more and laid the whip on the mare. My, how scared I was as we drove on it! Safely across, I asked how we'd ever get back and was told not to worry, it would be there for many years to come." As a matter of fact, it passed safely through several more floods and was finally taken down, in perfectly safe condition, to be replaced by a wider bridge, better suited to the amount of traffic.

The most serious danger to bridges in flood-time is the wreckage floating downstream with battering-ram action; barns, houses, and especially other bridges that have been washed off their foundations to float down intact. In 1850 a railroad bridge was built across the Connecticut at Bellows Falls. It was a sturdy structure of two spans with a solidly-built granite pier in midstream. In a freshet a highway bridge came floating along, erect and whole. When it struck the railroad bridge the lattice

Fig. 51: THREE-MILE BRIDGE, OTTER CREEK, MIDDLEBURY
Showing reinforcement with laminated arches

trusses folded up like an accordion but its ridgepole pierced the boarded sides, projecting far on the downstream side. As soon as the wreckage had come to a temporary rest, daring men ran out and cut it free, thus saving the railroad bridge from any serious damage. Twenty years later the increased size and weight of freight trains made its replacement necessary, but it was found to be in perfectly sound condition.

Always experimenting, bridge builders were never at a loss to find ways of strengthening highway bridges damaged by floods or not strong enough to carry increased loads. Three-mile bridge near Middlebury (fig. 50) was built at a wide part of Otter Creek a little below the entrance of the Middlebury river. Age had weakened the long span by 1859

Fig. 52: LEWIS CREEK BRIDGE, NORTH FERRISBURG
Solid concrete replaces old stonework

and the floor sagged a few inches. Deacon Boyce was called in to fix it and he added the big laminated arches (fig. 51) in the summer of 1859 or 1860. The Deacon had a sharp eye for new ideas. It is said that he developed an unusual and successful manner of framing bridge floors by studying the underparts of freight cars when the new railroad came to town.

Some bridge builders were better carpenters than masons. Many of the old bridges rest on shore supports of stone piled up like stone walls in a pasture, with huge stones at the bottom and smaller ones at the top. These were laid "dry," without any mortar, and were a source of danger from

Fig. 53: VILLAGE BRIDGE AT NEWFANE
An unusual portal design

floods. Modern bridge builders, using portland cement which will harden in the presence of water as lime-mortar will not, are apt to replace the stonework with solid concrete. This has been done with the Lewis creek bridge at North Ferrisburg (fig. 52). The Newfane village bridge (fig. 53) was built in 1841 and its abutments of mortarless rocks have held it up for a century. Although attractive in appearance, it has now been replaced because of the sharp right-angled turns at the approaches. Its portal is of a design almost unique in Vermont.

Fig. 54: POST MILLS BRIDGE, THETFORD

Laying a dry wall is a special craft, and there are few who can do as good a job as shows in the abutments of the Post Mills bridge in Thetford (fig. 54). The lack of mortar seems to have made no trouble, small flat stones artfully hammered into the chinks having made an acceptable substitute. The ravages of time and frost, and the heavy ice which batters the abutments during the spring freshets, make repairs necessary sooner or

Fig. 55: UPPER BRIDGE, EAST CHARLOTTE
Showing pointing of old stonework

later. One method of repair is "pointing," or forcing cement mortar into the joints of the stonework. This has been done in the upper bridge at East Charlotte (fig. 55). Where the masonry is solid this makes a satisfactory job because it binds the surface stones, which absorb most of the blows, into one mass.

Under certain conditions pointing may not suffice. The face stones may not be securely bonded into the backing, or perhaps the backing is inferior material like rounding "hardheads" from the stream bed, which tend to shift. In such a case it is wise to do something more elaborate. The Comstock bridge in Montgomery (fig. 56) has one of the abutments pointed, but the other cased in a thin concrete wall, the mixture having

Fig. 56: COMSTOCK BRIDGE, TROUT RIVER, MONTGOMERY VILLAGE
Showing concrete facing of old stonework

been forced into the open joints of the stonework as the concrete was poured. This has made a permanent job at low cost. This bridge was built in 1883 by the Jewett brothers who constructed most of the bridges in the neighborhood. Montgomery has more covered wooden bridges still in use than any other town in the state. All of them are fine examples of the bridge-builders' art, and most of them have the good luck to be situated in especially beautiful scenery. It is a town that the bridge-lover should visit. He will find the old bridges well maintained, many of them showing wise modern practise for their preservation, preventive work that is used in the neighboring town of Enosburg as well, as illustrated in the bridge between the two villages (fig. 57).

Fig. 57: SHINGLE MILL BRIDGE, ENOSBURG
Between West and East Enosburg

When our forefathers had a bridge to build they did not make an elaborate set of drawings as we do today; they might have but a rough sketch to go by, but usually they planned the details of the bridge as it grew. If they had any experimenting to do, any guessing about the design of the truss, it was done with models. One of Nicholas Powers' bridge models is displayed in his grandson Powers' store in Pittsford, a precious relic. Sometimes these models were made for the builder's own pleasure; occasionally to show to a building committee if there was competition for a job. Lemuel Chenoweth, a well known bridge engineer of Beverley, Virginia, was one of many competitors for the bridge over Tygart's river at Philippi, West Virginia. Some of the Yankees present had models of perfect form, painted in the highest art. Chenoweth's model drew little attention until he set it between two chairs as abutments and stood on it, calling on the others to put theirs to the same test. He was awarded the contract!

There was little competition in Vermont. The selectmen usually went to some craftsman whose successful work was known to them and dickered about price and materials. Their specifications were simple; perhaps to follow the type of another bridge, usually to define the size. "A load of hay wide and high" sufficed for dimensions. Native pine was much used, but as it was less durable when exposed to dampness or spray, either hemlock or spruce were favorite materials. Powers once stated that a spruce stick (the strongest of the three woods) was capable of carrying the same load as an equal weight of iron. This may have been true before the days of rolled steel sections. It was argument enough for him when backed by the low cost of the abundant supplies of timber.

Contractors were fussy about their timber. It had to be good sound clear stuff, thoroughly air-seasoned for two or three years before use. Some of the busier men had their own sawmills so they were always sure of ample supplies for proper material. The lack of it often explains the delay in rebuilding a wrecked bridge.

No Vermont highway bridges were built by great engineers like Burr or Howe. With the exception of a few men such as Granger and Powers, the builders were men hardly known outside their own communities. They were skilled craftsmen, to be sure, but self-taught, self-reliant, natural-born engineers and more worthy of respect for that reason. Such men neither needed nor wanted the elaborate blueprints used today. A level meadow was their drafting-board; saw, chisel and auger their instruments. Experience had taught them the sizes of timbers needed. Caution and convenience dictated that they be big enough. It may have been wasteful by modern engineering standards, but wood was plentiful and cheap.

David Stevenson, a Scottish engineer who visited this country to study our methods, wrote in his book:—"The timbers of the bridges are fitted together on the ground previous to their erection on the piers. They are again taken asunder and each piece is put up separately in the place which it is to occupy, by means of a scaffolding of timber." This brief explanation is clear, but worth amplifying.

An open field was usually close to the bridge. Here the timbers were laid on the grassy ground. A sample "panel" or part of the frame was laid out carefully by the master builder who was so concerned with accuracy that he marked his joints with a sharp knife-blade, as a pencil line was too coarse. All his skill, all the secrets of his craft, went into this initial operation. Patterns or "templates" were copied from this sample with the greatest exactness, to be used by his men in cutting the joints. They worked with fine-toothed saws and keen chisels for greater accuracy. The design of the truss may have been made "by guess," but its execution "by gosh" would have led to nothing but failure. Truss joints had to be really exact, not merely "good enough." The scarf-joints with which the long stringers were spliced had to bear at every portion of their surfaces so when the hardwood "keys" or wedges were driven home they would be, in effect, one long, solid timber. Any considerable error in making the joints meant a settlement, a sag, when the falsework or scaffolding was taken away. Even a trifling error caused a gradual settling later, the weakening of a truss, and a shorter life for the bridge.

Wooden pins (fig. 58) connected the parts. These were called treenails (pronounced "trunnels") and were made of oak. Most builders soaked or boiled them in oil to assure durability. The great truss-timbers were carefully arranged on the grass and leveled, and holes were bored with big augers to receive the pins. Here, again, accuracy was essential if the parts were to fit exactly in place when erected. This necessity for an accuracy now used only in fine cabinet-work is perhaps one reason for saying that bridge-building is a lost art. It is not. There are still plenty of

Fig. 58: LATTICE AND TREENAILS
Otter Creek Bridge, Ferrisburg

men competent to build wooden bridges with old-time accuracy combined with modern improvements in construction.

While this work was going on in the meadow a scaffolding or falsework was erected in the stream between the waiting abutments. On this the finished bridge timbers were set up, supported by it until the last key or treenail was driven home. The first timbers laid were the stringers, those long pieces extending from bank to bank. These were never set level, but always with a "camber," so the midstream part was several inches higher than the ends. This camber was one of the bridge builder's evidences of skill, a secret of his craft. It had two uses. Undoubtedly, the more important is that a bridge will always settle a little when the falsework is removed, no matter how good the joints, and this comes out of the camber-allowance; also, the vibration of traffic may increase this settlement as time passes. The lesser reason has to do with the untrustworthiness of the human eye which sees a long level line as if it curved down in the middle. The camber corrects this. The Greeks knew it. They never built flights of level steps leading up to their temples; instead, these steps always had an upward curve in their middle called "entasis." It is synonymous with "camber" in horizontal members.

When the erection of the bridge was completed the falsework was demolished. This was the first test of the bridge. If all was well it would settle a little, compacting its parts into an enduring whole. If the builder had made an error of judgement or had failed to watch his men's accuracy of workmanship, there was real trouble.

Nicholas Powers, Vermont's most noted bridge builder, built his best-known bridge at North Blenheim, New York. It was of unusual design, of immense length for its single span. They called it "Powers' Folly" and many were the predictions that it would collapse when the falsework was removed. As the time approached to knock away the props the pessimists redoubled their croakings. "If she goes I'll go with her," said Powers as he climbed up onto the ridge. That reassured some, but others mourned that the bridge would sag so much of its own weight it would be useless for traffic. "If she sags an inch," Nick called down to the waiting crowd, "I'll jump off!" and directed that the last timbers of the falsework be knocked away. The bridge settled a tiny fraction of an inch, less than he had allowed for. His skill acknowledged, he became a popular hero.

North Blenheim folks have cherished their bridge since its erection in 1855. When the authorities decided it had to be replaced because of the sharp turns at its approaches, public sentiment compelled them to build a new bridge alongside the old. This was retained under the care of the county commissioners as a museum, the old bridge itself the chief exhibit.

Powers was a red-blooded man of good stock. The family traces back to one of William the Conqueror's knights, and conquest of difficulties was one of their characteristics. He was the eleventh son of an eleventh son and all of them were handy with tools. It may be said that "Nick" was born, not with a silver spoon in his mouth, but with saw and chisel in his fist! He had the reputation of being lucky, but his luck seems to have been a combination of shrewd foresight and meticulous accuracy. Born in 1817, when he died in 1897 he had built scores of bridges, large and small. The carpentry of heavy timbers was in the blood. His son, Charles, when only sixteen, worked at his father's side on the great bridge at Havre-de-Grace, Maryland, and was a respected bridge builder when he died at the early age of thirty years.

This Maryland bridge was a tough problem. It had been designed by professional engineers, but it showed signs of failing during construction. Powers was in charge of the workmen and was called in consultation by the Big Boss. He was asked if he were an engineer, and with more courage than accuracy, said he was. "How long will it take you to make a design for this bridge that will stand up?" was the next question. "It's nearly noon," said he, "I'll give it to you after I've had my dinner." By two o'clock he had covered the sides of a big balk of timber with sketches and calculations and called the authorities to inspect this unwieldly document. It did not take Nick long to convince them he could do what he promised. He was given the contract to finish the bridge. He set his gang of fifty men to work, and in due course the structure was completed successfully.

Meanwhile his wife in far away Vermont kept pestering him to come home where he was needed. He repeatedly quieted her with generous remittances and suggestions that she hire more help for the farm work. Finally, he agreed to get home for Thanksgiving. He finished the bridge ahead of time, thereby earning a $500 bonus, and wrote a five-word letter to his wife to tell her he was on his way. Not even waiting to be photographed with his gang on the new bridge during the opening ceremonies, he got back just in time for the turkey. Never again did he go so far from home.

Some Vermont bridges were built by young men with more self-assurance than experience, but they generally made good. Powers built his first bridge in 1837 at Pittsford Mills. Not yet twenty-one years old, he was too young to sign the contract, which his father took over for him. When the bridge was taken down in 1931 it was found to be so strong and sound that a twenty-ton steam roller was driven across it without hesitation. Although efforts were made to sell it to Henry Ford for his collection, his agents arrived too late to secure it.

Another ambitious youngster was less lucky with his first contract although during his life he built many other bridges that were successful and enduring. The late Caleb B. Lamson of South Newfane was a skilled carpenter before he was out of his 'teens. When he was twenty-two he was engaged to build his first bridge, a splendid one across West river near West Dummerston (fig. 59). The longest bridge in Windham county, its two spans total 280 feet in length. During construction the falsework gave way before enough of the bridge timbers had been placed to make it self-supporting. Lamson was on top, helping to secure the heavy timbers, when it began to go. He stayed on his midstream perch, watching to see which way the wreckage was going to fall, and jumped to the other side. He landed in shallow water, injuring his back permanently. His helper was instantly killed.

Vermonters have always been accustomed to pay as they go. If they want something they cannot afford, they do without. For a good many years the settlers in Brookfield had been compelled to reach the village by a roundabout journey if they happened to live on the hill farms to its north. A long narrow pond barred the way, a pond too wide to bridge with a single span and with a deep mud bottom that made piers impossible to construct. When winter set in people crossed on the ice, but with the arrival of the warm March winds they were reluctant to abandon the

Fig. 59: BRIDGE OVER WEST RIVER, WEST DUMMERSTON

short-cut; they took chances on the rotten ice. Daniel Belknap broke through and was drowned. Naturally, this tragedy revived the problem of bridging the pond.

About 1819 Luther Adams and some neighbors built a log bridge on the ice as a private enterprise, constructing it like a long, thin raft so it could be used as a crude pontoon bridge when the ice melted. This worked so well that in 1826 the town voted to take it over as a part of the road system. Crossing on this was an exciting experience. As long as the logs were dry it would float well enough even if it settled under heavy loads, but when they got watersoaked, the floor was wet even under a horse and rider. When this happened, another tier of logs was set on top of the first raft, followed in succession by other layers as the years passed.

Photo by Herbert Wheaton Congdon.

Fig. 60: THE FLOATING BRIDGE, BROOKFIELD

In 1884 Orlando Ralph had the bright idea of buoying up the raft with kerosene barrels under its floor. This worked, and the system has been used ever since. The present floating bridge (fig. 60) is called the sixth. It was built in 1935-36 by Brookfield and the state jointly, and makes use of tarred barrels chained together and tied against any side motion. The wooden part of the structure that is under water is creosoted to protect it from decay as long as possible. The roadway is a single one, flanked by sidewalks with outside railings where the village small fry congregate to fish for perch. At either end are ramps to take care of the rise and fall of the pond level. The bridge is 320 feet over all with 296 feet of it afloat. At one time there were five or six such floating bridges in

New England; this is thought to be the only one still in use in the entire country.

Vermonters get touchy if the federal government uses marble or granite from out of the state in our post offices; yet our state authorities used seventy-seven thousand board feet of creosoted *Oregon* fir in this bridge and nobody even suggested Vermont hemlock, so durable in damp places. Presumably there was a good reason, but it was not mentioned in the program for the celebration that was held in connection with the dedication festivities. It was a typical Vermont festival, with a pageant, land and water sports, and the inevitable speeches by public officials. A good band furnished music for the dance on the bridge, which was gay with colored electric lights that evening. The blessings of twentieth century progress were shed on nineteenth century inventiveness.

IV

PAYING THE PIPER

FINANCING as expensive a thing as a new bridge is a serious matter in Vermont. Taxes are high, and there is not much to tax, anyway. That is why so many early bridges were financed by lotteries, legalized by special acts of legislature. It was a painless way to raise money. It took little ready cash to buy a ticket and of course the buyer was pretty sure he would reap a rich reward. Strange to say, no stories have come down to us about the lucky folks. Probably, being thrifty Yankees, they put their winnings in the cracked teapot on the mantel; the others took good care to keep quiet. The majority of our highway bridges were short enough to make possible their erection out of town funds, raised, of course, by taxes levied by action of town meeting. That meant a good deal of discussion. Sometimes the matter went over to the next year's meeting.

Nearly a hundred years ago (stories live a long time in Vermont) the March meeting of Rutland town was discussing one of the articles in the "warning" that concerned a proposed new bridge. It took good speaking to get affirmative action, and the proponents seemed to have all the orators. Everything was going their way until a farmer arose and was recognized by the presiding officer. "We've built four bridges in this town," said he, "four bridges within two miles; now we are asked to build a fifth. Mr. Moderator, I move we bridge the whole dummed creek lengthwise."

Really big bridges were not within the means of the average small town with its tiny villages. Hence the lotteries. But lotteries were getting out of favor with the church-members just about the time that thrifty folks had begun to realize they wanted some safe way to invest their money. In that way toll bridges were ushered in to our country. If the bridge were not too big, one capitalist could finance it as he was pretty sure of a good return. Larger ones, such as spanned the Connecticut, were built by stock companies. In either case it meant a petition to the legislature which usually granted the necessary charter containing provisions to safeguard both the investor and the citizens who were to make use of the bridge.

The Guildhall-Lancaster toll bridge was erected under a charter issued by New Hampshire in 1804. The stock company consisted of twenty-two men, who held the forty shares between them. The par value of these was $50; as one man plunged to the extent of twelve shares none of the others held many. The charter provided for an allowable return of twelve per cent on the investment after maintenance charges were met. If the net return was found to be over this, as shown by the audit made every six years, the toll-rates were to be lowered; if it was under six per cent they were to be raised. This audit was made by the justices of the Superior Court. It seemed to be an eminently fair system. The profits in this case were never high enough for the rates to be lowered. Finally they became so low that the company sold out to the New Hampshire town of Lancaster and the two Vermont towns served by the bridge, Guildhall and Lunenburg. The bridge became free of tolls in 1894.

The old schedule of toll-rates is interesting to the motorists who carelessly hand a half-dollar to a sprucely-uniformed attendant:—

1. For each foot-passenger, 1 cent.
2. For each horse and rider, 4 cents.
3. For each chaise, chair, sulky, or other riding carriage drawn by one horse, 10 cents.
4. For each riding sleigh drawn by one horse, 5 cents.
5. For each coach, chariot, phaeton or other four-wheeled vehicle for passengers, drawn by more than one horse, 20 cents.

Fig. 61: GUILDHALL-LANCASTER BRIDGE ACROSS CONNECTICUT RIVER

6. For each curicle, 12 cents. (A two wheeled carriage, swankily drawn by a pair of horses.)
7. For each cart or other carriage of burthen, drawn by two beasts, 10 cents and 2 cents for each additional yoke of oxen or pair of horses.
8. For each horse, exclusive of those rid on, 3 cents.
9. For each neat creature, 1 cent.
10. For each sheep or swine, ½ cent, and to each team one person and no more shall be allowed as a driver to pass free of toll.

Lest it be thought that our forebears were encouraging slovenliness, the reference to "neat creatures" has nothing to do with curry-combs, brushes or braided tails. It refers to Mr. and Mrs. Cow and their progeny.

The present Guildhall bridge (fig. 61) is probably the third on the site.

Fig. 62: MOUNT ORNE BRIDGE, LUNENBURG-LANCASTER (1912)

It was built in 1840, which explains why the company did not make much money; they had two bridges to build out of income. The Vermont side of the river has only two tiny villages which depend on Lancaster for most of their commerce. That New Hampshire town also serves Vermont by the Mount Orne bridge (fig. 62) which connects it with Lunenburg a few miles farther upstream. This bridge was built by New Hampshire with Vermont's financial aid in 1912, one of the newest covered wooden bridges. The cost was $5,000 and no construction company was employed. The brothers Babbitt, New Hampshire men, took charge of the work under the supervision of the selectmen of the two towns.

Far up in the northeastern corner of Vermont, with only the pie-shaped town of Canaan between it and the Canadian border, Lemington faces

Fig. 63: COLUMBIA BRIDGE, CONNECTICUT RIVER, LEMINGTON (1912)

New Hampshire's town of Columbia across the Connecticut river, a small stream here. The Babbitts also built the present Columbia bridge, in 1912; the second new-old bridge within a year. Lemington has no villages and only about 150 inhabitants; it lacks even a post-office, being served from New Hampshire. Nevertheless, it has heavy and valuable forests on its mountains, and so was able to share the cost of the new bridge with Columbia. Public subscriptions helped to finance it, too. Columbia bridge, as it is called (fig. 63) was originally a toll bridge as was the Mount Orne one. The first bridge at this site was wrecked by a gale; the second, built about a hundred years ago, was burned when the toll buildings were set afire by sparks from a locomotive. There was no fire-fighting equipment on hand, so the fire spread to the bridge and destroyed it.

The present bridge, the third, is free of tolls and is a fine example of

Fig. 64: BEDELL'S BRIDGE OVER THE CONNECTICUT AT NEWBURY

modern science applied to building an old-fashioned bridge. Wood is used for the trusses but they are stiffened by steel rods and bolts, a concession to twentieth century ways. The old split granite abutments were kept, and strengthened by encasing them in concrete. One side is boarded up for better protection from the weather, but the other is half open, for light.

Lower down the Connecticut the old bridges are being rapidly replaced by modern structures; better for motor traffic but lacking in picturesque charm. The old toll bridge at Newbury (fig. 64), often called Bedell's bridge. is one of these relics. Engineers find it interesting as a good example of what they call the "Burr-arch" truss, especially as it was constructed as late as 1866, when most Vermont builders were using more modern types.

Windsor toll bridge is one of the two remaining toll bridges across the Connecticut and holds the record for collecting tolls for the longest time, now 150 years. The first bridge was built in 1796, one of those that came into being as a result of Colonel Hale's successful feat at Bellows Falls. A spring freshet carried it away in 1824. It was replaced as quickly as possible, but the second bridge met the same fate as its predecessor in 1849. The undaunted proprietors built a third and again suffered loss by the flood of March, 1866. The fourth and present bridge was built that same year by James Tasker, and so far has defied the floods and hurricanes that have devastated the Connecticut valley. The first two bridges were three-span affairs. The third and also the present one were constructed with two spans. The total length is 468 feet; a long bridge for our neighborhood.

Old reports to the stockholders present some interesting statistics that shed light on the conditions of their times. Before railroads changed the picture, a large part of the bridge's revenue came from tolls on cattle being driven to market. The peak of this traffic was in the prosperous quarter-century beginning in 1824, with the building of the second bridge. In 1838, an especially good year for the proprietors, 14,084 sheep and 2,208 cattle paid tolls on their way to market. The coming of the railroads and development of the Chicago dressed-meat business rapidly cut into that source of revenue, however. Among the early toll-collectors was one Brown and there are a number of interesting entries in his record-book. In 1825 he notes the passage of Lafayette on his last visit to the United States; in 1831 there is mention of a wolf-hunting party crossing the bridge. If all these old books could be gathered in one place, what fascinating sidelights they would cast on the way our forefathers lived!

Statements differ about the feeling of the public towards the old Windsor-Cornish bridge properties. One authority says that no unreasonable

Fig. 65: WINDSOR TOLL BRIDGE

rates have ever been charged and there has never been strong talk of asking the two states to purchase and free the bridge. Another is equally sure that in earlier days at least, there was considerable criticism of the management. It mentions particularly James Monteith, a toll-collector with one eye on the main chance. He was an inveterate knitter, his hands never idle as he sat waiting for customers.

He devised a way to prevent interruptions in his work by compounding the tolls of the larger families who used the bridge frequently, so they paid a monthly sum. This he set arbitrarily, between two dollars and fifteen dollars, according to his pleasure. Privileged characters of that sort were passed by a nod of the knitter's head. One day a woman, not of these favored few, attempted to pass without paying, as she felt the toll was exorbitant. James reached up from his knitting, loosed the rope, and the gate (fig. 65) promptly fell. It caught on the shafts between the buggy and the frightened horse, who did his best to kick it to bits. "Make up your mind, lady, which side of the river you want to stay on *and stay there!*" he said, clicking his needles. Troubled in conscience, she paid her toll and the cost of repairs to the gate as well. James Monteith kept on knitting.

Toll bridges did good business on Saturday nights if there was a drinking-place on one side of the river and not the other. Some of the collectors, as an obvious precaution, charged round-trip tolls to those who were accustomed to return with empty pockets and uncertain footsteps. Others were sometimes put to considerable inconvenience. An overloaded pedestrian returned early Sunday morning and hazily realized he was about to cross the toll bridge. Standing unsteadily before the collector's door he began to bellow, "Come and get your toll or I'll run your bridge!" As the keeper had no intention of getting out of a nice warm bed for two cents, the hilarious one, after loud and repeated warnings, ran the bridge. Progress was difficult. His legs didn't track. Having reached the other end, they turned him about and carried him back again. Stubborn conscience compelled him to repeat his stentorian warning to the gate-keeper, who still kept to his bed. Again he wove his unsteady way across; this time he sat down to ponder the matter. It dawned over him that he had to cross a bridge if he were to reach his home, so back he went. To his amazement, he found himself on the wrong side. There was the toll-house, silent and dark. It was the proper place to pay toll; so he aroused the echos if not the collector with his threats to run the bridge if that official did not take his two coppers. Crossing, re-crossing and proclaiming, he wore away the night. When day dawned the stubborn toll-collector yielded, collected his due and led the conscientious one across for the last time, starting him up the hill towards the haven where he would be.

A convivial soul lived down Vernon way who was much given to practical jokes. Once he bet a gallon of rum that he could get by the parsimonious guardian of the Brattleboro toll bridge without paying. His friends took him up. Waiting until the toll gatherer had gone into the village on an errand, Barney approached the toll-gate on a trot, but instead of running the bridge he turned into the toll-house kitchen where the collector's wife was frying griddle-cakes. Barney jogged around the kitchen, saying nothing, and sat down on a chair in a dark corner, looking as much like an idiot as possible. Watching the cook, he finally asked, "What are them things?" The woman explained they were cakes, and good to eat. A hospitable soul, she went further and passed him the plate of cakes already fried. Barney jumped up, pulled his shirt out of his trousers to make an apron into which he dumped the entire plateful. Without a word he jogged around the kitchen once more, out of the door and across the bridge. "I'd break his head," said a neighbor who had seen the whole performance. "Oh, the poor fellow," said the deluded cook, "he doesn't know what he's about; let him go."

One of our smaller toll bridges was owned by an unusually thrifty citizen who kept his rates so close to the upper limit that people acquainted with the place made use of the approaches to the former ferry in winter time, crossing on the ice. Naturally, this annoyed him. He remembered the Biblical injunction to "Take the foxes, the little foxes that spoil the vines" and laid his plans. Securing a quantity of salt, he sowed it liberally on the ice where the current kept it thin. Before the salt had completed its work his own hired man came along, driving his employer's team hitched to a load of wood. Rather than disturb the boss to raise the gate, he took the road across the ice. When he reached the salted place the whole rig crashed through. Horses, sled and load were swept under the ice by the current and the driver barely escaped with his life.

Freeing the chartered bridges from tolls is a comparatively new thing. The first of the Connecticut river bridges to be made free, however, was

Fig. 66: PRIVATE BRIDGE OVER WINOOSKI RIVER, MARSHFIELD

Fig. 67: PRIVATE BRIDGE, OTTER CREEK, NEAR BRANDON

that between Norwich, Vermont and Hanover, New Hampshire, July 1, 1859. It was an occasion for great rejoicing, marked by a celebration with speeches and music. One of the speakers, Professor Sanborn, declared that "toll-gates are contrary to the genius of our free institutions and are tolerated only from necessity." In view of this feeling, so prevalent among Vermonters, it is interesting to note the new trend back to the old method of finance. Sometimes it works out to the benefit of the investors; sometimes the state has to take over.

The pioneers' system of neighbor-help-neighbor has been carried over into modern days. If the bridge-company cannot swing their investment, the state steps in. Our democratic town-meetings have gone a bit further,

Fig. 68: "OLD '76 BRIDGE" NEAR RUTLAND COUNTRY CLUB
View before restoration to show construction

for there is a tradition stronger than law that makes it obligatory on the town to furnish a good road to a homestead, even if it means a bridge, too. If the bridge is big enough, it is covered to conserve a considerable investment. That explains a covered bridge like the one in Marshfield (fig. 66). It is not certain that such bridges were built for the use of only one family. There are good many that once served several families but, as farms were abandoned, have lapsed to that status. A few covered bridges have always been private ones, privately built, owned, and maintained. Such is the one over Otter Creek between Brandon and Sudbury (fig. 67) which connects two parts of a large farm and never led to a homestead.

A good many people complain bitterly when "they" replace a fine old bridge with a commonplace modern structure, forgetting that under our town-meeting system they have both opportunity and duty to speak out against what is termed "vandalism." It is an encouraging sign that a group of people who appreciate the old bridges saved one from destruction in Rutland very recently. Near the country club, on a little used road, stands a bridge affectionately termed "Old '76" (fig. 68). It is not very old—it was built in 1876—but it is very picturesque. The glamor of steel and concrete, the erroneous belief that they are everlasting and the desire to do the usual thing, led to a decision to replace this with a modern structure because the old bridge was showing weakness in its floor-structure, the weak point in so many wooden bridges. This interested minority set to work. They aroused the newspapers and their readers. They sat down with the highway engineers and set them to figuring. The result was a thorough and practical modern repair job to an old bridge. Now everyone is satisfied. Some of the truss-timbers had decayed, due to neglect, to lack of proper maintenance. These were replaced with new ones, using treenails to secure them, some old, some new. Concrete retaining walls were built at the ends to keep damp earth away from the wood, the gap spanned by iron plates. The rotted floor stringers were replaced by steel girders and a new floor was installed. Every precaution was taken to keep water out from places where it would do harm. Finally, the roof was re-shingled and the sides re-boarded. The illustration is purposely from a picture made when the neglected bridge was ready for condemnation and is used because it shows its anatomy so well. Give Father Time a few years and the old favorite will look natural again. Amusingly enough, a huge motor-transport loaded with automobiles lost its way recently and crossed the old-new bridge with neither difficulty nor danger. It is indeed encouraging that a few energetic people could accomplish such a valuable deed for their community. It should give courage to others.

   A curiosity which might be seen in Vermont is a modern stream-lined locomotive drawing a train of air-conditioned cars through an old-fashioned covered wooden railroad bridge. There are not many such left. We

Fig. 69: ST. JOHNSBURY & LAKE CHAMPLAIN R. R., HARDWICK

have seven of the twenty-nine remaining in the entire country; a rapid change from the beginning of the present century when the Boston & Maine alone had over a hundred. The Pioneer Junction bridge near Barre is the only one on the little Montpelier & Wells River road, the St. Johnsbury & Lake Champlain having another five, one of which is near Hardwick (fig. 69). Covered wooden railroad bridges are apt to be ungainly in proportion. Only one track wide, they are of necessity much taller than a highway bridge of similar width, because of the clearance needed by the locomotives. The engineer who planned the Pioneer Junction bridge-portal was a skilful designer, and has given considerable distinction to its portal. The Hardwick bridge, whether by accident

Fig. 70: BRIDGE ACROSS MISSISQUOI RIVER IN SWANTON

or a sense of puckish humor, has an amusing resemblance to the cars that pass through it.

Vermont's longest covered railroad bridge is in Swanton (fig. 70) crossing the Missisquoi river. A three-span bridge with plain rectangular portals, it might pass for a tall highway bridge if it were not for the three ventilators on the roof. These carry off part of the smoke, the rest escaping through the long unboarded strip under the eaves. There is little enough smoke to escape these days. Trains over this bridge are so infrequent that it is said every time one is scheduled to cross it, the station agents give a formal party. The railroads have slim pickings now. The necessary for economy may explain the continued existence of these wooden bridges. Their youth is their most amazing characteristics; the engineering department of the railroads owning them state that the Swanton bridge was built in 1898, the Pioneer Junction one in 1904 and that near Hardwick in 1908, making them much newer than the usual estimates.

Younger members of a railroad's engineering staff do not always welcome criticism or suggestion from laymen, especially if they are old. A bright young man was sent by a certain company to take charge of the construction of an unimportant bridge over a quiet little stream. Near by was the homestead of an old man who was deeply interested in watching the work. One day, worried by what he saw, he called on the youngster to tell him, as tactfully as possible, that his bridge span was too short to accommodate the stream when swollen with spring freshets. The younger man listened with scant patience and finally sent old John about his business rather brusquely. "Young man," he said as he left, "God Almighty sends His waters where He wills. That bridge will be washed away." Sure enough, it went out the following spring and two more attempts were made by the railroad folks before they admitted the old man was right.

Fig. 71: BRIDGE OVER WINOOSKI RIVER, EAST MONTPELIER

V

CALLING THE TUNE

ONE of the old bridge builders was asked how he knew that a bridge was strong enough. "I watch it when a drove of cattle crosses," said he. For several reasons that is a good test. A fat steer may weigh nearly three quarters of a ton, cattle huddle together when being driven across a dark bridge, and what is more, a moving load is a greater strain on a bridge than a stationary one. If a bridge made no complaints in its many joints the builder knew it could carry considerably more than such a test load. No wonder our old bridges have proved safe for modern traffic of a weight and speed of which their builders never dreamed. This extra strength is what our engineers call the "factor of safety." It is an allowance for unforeseen emergencies. Today, engineers take into account not only the expected floor load, but also wind-pressure from winter's gales. Then they allow something more for possible hurricanes. They figure the usual snow load and add to it for the off chance of a fall of deep wet snow.

The *Political Observer,* a newspaper published in Walpole, New Hampshire, printed an item under date-line of Brattleboro, December 1, 1804, which read, "On Tuesday last the new toll bridge over the Connecticut river which connects Brattleboro with Hinsdale, New Hampshire, was opened for passengers. The bridge does the highest honor to Mr. Kingsley, the architect as well as to Mr. Lovel Kelton and the mechanics who executed the work under their direction.

"It has been pronounced to have been erected upon the best plan of any yet put into execution in this part of the Union, combining greater strength with less weight of material and promising more durability."

The same paper says on February 16, 1805:—"We learn that on Thursday last the new bridge lately erected across the Connecticut river between Brattleboro and Hinsdale fell and was crushed to ruins. The cause is said to have been the great weight of snow lodged on it."

Faith in the new plan had not been warranted, or perhaps there had not been sufficient allowance for unexpected burdens. In fairness to the designer it should be emphasized that this happened long before the days of testing laboratories or the scientific analysis of stresses and strains developed in truss-members. Kingsley had to do his experimenting with small scale models. The wealth of data available to modern engineers did not exist in 1804. He was an experimenter and his experiment failed. Other inventors of his time were more fortunate.

Pioneer builders not only invented new trusses; they had to invent words, names for the parts of these new trusses. A truss is defined as "an assemblage of members so combined as to form a rigid framework." It is used to carry a bridge where only an "assemblage of members" could support the load of so long a span. Naturally, there are many kinds of trusses to suit the conditions and materials. Some are very old, dating far back in history. The oldest, the "simple truss," is a triangle, for that geometric figure is the only one that cannot change its shape without altering the length of its sides. It is seldom seen except in its early development, the "kingpost truss" which is found in the smaller bridges like that over Pine Brook in Waitsfield (fig. 72). A little reflection will show that the horizontal member of the triangle, the "bottom chord," carries the floor load and therefore tends to sag down. The kingpost, strongly framed into this, takes the load up to the point of the "A" which the truss resembles. Here it is also firmly secured. The kingpost is therefore in "tension" as the engineers say, the weight of the floor pulling it down. The sloping parts of the "A" carry the load down to their ends, and are in "compression." They are stiffened by diagonal "struts" from their middles to the bottom of the kingpost. Owing to the characteristics of wood,

Fig. 72: KINGPOST TRUSS, PINE BROOK BRIDGE, WAITSFIELD
The bottom chord is beneath the floor

the end joints of the kingpost are danger points, so it is often replaced by an iron tie-rod which can be set without cutting away much wood at the joints.

Practical considerations limit the kingpost truss to short spans. The "queenpost truss" is used for those somewhat longer, but not for really long spans. Like its masculine relative, the queenpost truss is of ancient lineage. Imagine a kingpost truss twenty feet long sliced in half vertically and the halves pulled ten feet apart. Then make the bottom "chord" or timber thirty feet long, set on it two "queenposts" connecting the points of the half-A's with it, join the queenposts at the top with an upper chord, and the result is a queenpost truss (fig. 73). The space between the queen-

Fig. 73: LAMOILLE RIVER BRIDGE, WOLCOTT
A Queenpost Truss

posts and the chords is often occupied by "struts" or braces like an inverted V. These show in the Wolcott bridge and also in the one at Lyndon (fig. 74) on the road from Lyndonville to Kirby. The queenpost truss was sometimes varied in its details. The Miller Brook bridge in Stowe (fig. 75) shows what may be called a queenpost truss with X-shaped braces occupying its middle panel. A purist would give this a different name; he would call it a Warren truss. Why be too meticulous?

The simple styles of trusses appeared mostly in the humbler bridges, the small ones that lacked roofs but had their trusses boarded in. They are not strong enough for really long spans, but did good service in the places to which they were suited. Most of them still in use have iron rods

Fig. 74: CROSSING PASSUMPSIC RIVER, LYNDONVILLE TO KIRBY
Another type of Queenpost Truss

in place of the wooden king- and queen-posts and iron bolts to secure the joints. Some of these bridges now have roofs added.

If a bridge is to withstand floods and freshets it is best designed in a single span from bank to bank. Midstream piers are apt to be sorely battered by floating debris, ice, and the scurrying boulders washed along the bottom by the unusual rush of water. Obviously, the higher it is set above the water, the safer it is from water-borne trees and other flotsam. But the higher it is, the farther back it must start from the gently-sloping banks, for stone abutments extending into the stream would endanger the bridge by narrowing the passageway at the very time the swollen stream needs width. That means a longer bridge. To meet these conditions, new trusses had to be devised to make long spans possible.

Fig. 75: MILLER BROOK BRIDGE, STOWE
Warren Truss

One of the first was invented and patented by Theodore Burr, who became famous for the railroad and highway bridges he constructed from Maine to Maryland. He was a skilful and ingenious engineer who combined sound theory with practical ability. He also had a positive genius for leadership. One of his first bridges to become famous was built in 1804 across the Hudson at Waterford, New York It was still carrying its traffic successfully when destroyed by fire in July, 1909, the longest-lived large bridge in the country. There is grim humor in the fact that the fire was caused by defective insulation of electric wires which set alight gas from a leaky main!

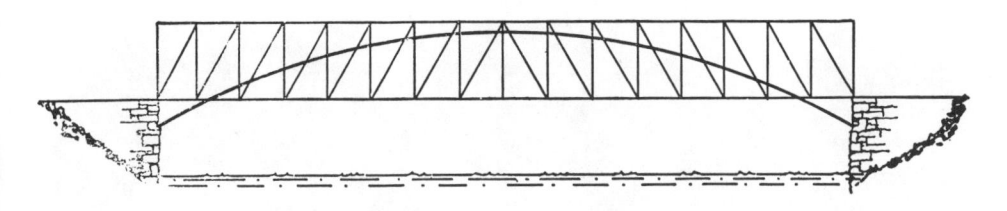

Fig. 76: DIAGRAM, BURR TRUSS AS USED IN CAMBRIDGE BRIDGE
An all-wood truss

Fig. 77: DOUBLE-LANE BRIDGE, CAMBRIDGE VILLAGE

Fig. 78: INTERIOR OF CAMBRIDGE VILLAGE BRIDGE, LAMOILLE RIVER
Sturdy arches and staunch overhead framing

He used in this bridge the combined truss and arch which he patented thirteen years later, in 1817, after he had erected several bridges in which he had experimented with variations. This all-wood "Burr-arch" truss was held in high favor for well over half a century (fig. 76), but was varied considerably in detail from his type. Vermont's nearest approach to a Burr-arch truss is in the Cambridge village bridge (fig. 77), one of the double-lane bridges now so rare. This bridge was built about 1845, after many discussions in town meetings. The arch does not foot as far below the stringer as usual, because it had to be kept above danger from floating debris. Nevertheless, the bridge is not only amply strong for its

Photo by Prof. George H. Perkins.

Fig. 79: FORMER HUBBELL'S FALLS BRIDGE, ESSEX

load, but has been sturdy enough to withstand many floods and gales. The water rose seven feet above its floor in the flood of 1927, but the old bridge stood firm. The light but staunch overhead framing has increased its durability (fig. 78) by bracing it laterally.

The Pulpmill bridge in Middlebury (fig. 12) was once much like this, but apparently it developed some weakness, and had to be stiffened with big laminated arches above the hewn ones, an addition never needed by the Cambridge bridge. Modified Burr trusses were used in a good many of our older bridges some of which have been destroyed. One of these spanned the Winooski at Hubbell's Falls (fig. 79) in a picturesque loca-

Photo by Clayton J. Fuller.

Fig. 80: SAFFORD BRIDGE, PLEASANT VALLEY, CAMBRIDGE

tion. By a curious trick of weathering, which may show very faintly in the illustration, the arch is outlined on the boarding of the sides.

Our bridge builders, practical men but not engineers, seldom followed the exact design of a truss. They looked it over, considered the materials they had at hand, and varied it to suit themselves. The result seems to have been good as far as durability goes, but it makes it difficult to give identifying names to their trusses. Competent mechanics with no great love of precedent, their output often puzzles the most skilled engineer to classify. In at least one case the truss defied analysis by modern means, and the needed repairs were made after experimenting with a model in the good old way!

Fig. 81: SAFFORD BRIDGE, CAMBRIDGE, FROM BROOK BED

If a bridge stands the test of time perhaps we should not be too critical of peculiarities in its design. Ingenious but unlettered bridge builders occasionally produced a truss that is frankly a mongrel with as many ancestral lines as a yellow dog. Such a bridge has stood for many years in the town of Cambridge (fig. 81) in the neighborhood called Pleasant Valley, almost in the shadow of Mount Mansfield. Here a queenpost truss is straddled by a big arch which is further aided by assisting struts underneath the bottom chord. It is high above the brook, safe from flood damage, and unconventional as its construction is, there is no question of its strength and longevity.

The Burr truss, if the name is to be accurately used, includes the arch

Fig. 82: UPPER BRIDGE, NORTH BRANCH BLACK RIVER, WEATHERSFIELD
A truss with alternating posts and sloping braces

which was the important part of his patent. A good many of the shorter bridges were designed without this arch, although using the familiar truss that went with his arch. This was usually built in Vermont with alternating posts and sloping braces. The braces slope inward from the portals to the middle post, which naturally has a brace on each side of it. It is an excellent truss if the joints of the posts are sufficiently strong. They are in tension, so their joints are danger points. The truss has no specific name and is more characteristic of old bridges than the later ones. There are

Fig. 83: BRIDGE ACROSS BROAD BROOK, ROYALTON

many good examples, two of which are illustrated in the bridges in Weathersfield and Royalton (figs. 82, 83).

Burr's letter to the builder of his Waterford bridge is among the papers of the historical society in Lancaster, Pennsylvania. Written in 1815 while he was building a remarkable bridge across the Susquehanna at McCalls Ferry, Pennsylvania, it gives a striking picture of the man. Never complaining of his troubles with flood, storm and winter cold, he constantly stresses the loyalty and zeal of his men. "They were in freezing water up to their armpits forty times each, on an average, every day" for a couple of weeks, but never complained of the long hours of labor. His enthusiasm was contagious. People who flocked from the surrounding countryside to watch the work gladly volunteered to help. "Between early January and the first part of February there were from 40 to 120 men freely giving their help each day," he writes and states with approval that "although liquor was handed in great abundance there were but two persons during the whole time that were in the least intoxicated."

Theodore Burr was born in Torringford, Connecticut, although he is occasionally mentioned as a Massachusetts man. The records seem to confuse him with an earlier child of the same given name who may have died in infancy. The date of his birth is therefore uncertain; it was probably August 16, 1771. He died in 1822 in Pennsylvania, only five years after he had patented the truss that bears his name. In 1789 he was married. His wife is said to have been the daughter of Captain Cook, the famous navigator. The story fails to tell how and where they met! Burr's life was a short one, but he left his mark in the world.

The bridge truss that is most frequently seen in Vermont is known as the "lattice" truss. Although there is some question as to its origin, it was patented in 1820 by Ithiel Town, an architect of New Haven, Connecticut. He took out a second patent on an improved form in 1835. This used secondary chords, spaced a little way from the principal ones. It is shown so well in the illustration of the Shingle mill bridge near East Enosburg (fig. 84) that further description seems superfluous. The planks of which it is made vary in size with the requirements of the bridge and are set in a lattice pattern, with the "chords," the long horizontal members, at top and bottom. The whole structure is fastened together with wooden pins of treenails to form a rigid mass. This truss has many advantages which were quickly recognized. It is easy to build, because of the simple sizes of lumber required and the small amount of fitting needed. It needs nothing but wood for its construction. An additional advantage is that this type of truss will stand more abuse from service than any other and will give evidence of distress long before its collapses. No wonder it grew

Fig. 84: INTERIOR, SHINGLE MILL BRIDGE NEAR EAST ENOSBURG
Town Lattice truss with secondary chords; lower main chord is beneath the floor line

in popularity so that it is used in more than twice as many of Vermont's bridges as any other type of truss. Although generally found in the larger bridges, it was used in a good many small ones also, with lighter timbers in the latticework and often without the secondary chords (fig. 85). Usually in the smaller bridges only one treenail is used at a joint, as two might weaken the lattice timber; obviously a less rigid piece of work.

No truss is perfect. Engineers say that the weakness of the Town lattice truss is its tendency to warp and get out of line if the overhead lateral bracing is insufficient. Some of our bridges were built by men who did not know their craft as well as did the recognized masters. Their errors in judgment showed up in time. The village bridge in Fairfax (fig. 86) leans

Fig. 85: TAFT BROOK BRIDGE, WESTFIELD
A small bridge with a light lattice truss

rather drunkenly, because of inadequate bracing, poor joints or some other avoidable cause. It is stronger than it looks, if one can judge from experience in demolition of supposedly weak bridges. Here is a sample from a score of reports. The contractor for the removal of the bridge took off the boarding and of course, the roof structure with its lateral bracing which is so important to the stiffness of the trusses. With very little effort the trusses were pushed several feet out of plumb, but having reached that point a powerful tractor with block and tackle was unable to pull them over. They had to be taken down piece by piece, stubbornly doing their duty to the end.

Fig. 86: FAIRFAX VILLAGE BRIDGE ACROSS MILL BROOK
It leans sideways, weary with age

A combination of the familiar lattice truss with Burr's arch is unusual, although lattice trusses have frequently been stiffened by the addition of laminated arches, technically a very different thing. The Mead bridge in Proctor (figs. 87, 88) appears to have been built with a lattice truss to which an arch of segmental hewn timbers was added at the start. The re-

Fig. 87: MEAD BRIDGE, OTTER CREEK, PROCTOR

sult is a hybrid of Burr and Town trusses. This bridge was built in 1840 by Nicholas M. Powers, Daniel C. Powers and Abraham Owen, which probably accounts for the combination of trusses. Powers had a great liking for the arch and Owen wanted to use the Town truss, which had not been tried in this locality before. Men of strong opinions, they apparently compromised by each having his own way. Mead bridge was built in 1840. Evidently its builders got on well together, for in 1842 they were commissioned to build the Gorham bridge (fig. 7), also across Otter Creek. Here there was no compromise; the Town lattice truss was employed. The town of Pittsford included both these bridges in its boundaries originally, but when part of it was set off for the new town of Proctor Mead bridge was in the new town which also included half of Gorham

Fig. 88: INTERIOR, MEAD BRIDGE, PROCTOR
Burr's arch combined with a Town truss

bridge in its limits. Both the Gorham bridge and Pittsford's Hammond bridge floated off their foundations in the flood of 1927. Both were built with Town's trusses and both were towed back and reset; an evidence of Owen's good judgment. Pittsford paid for resetting its bridge, but Proctor generously paid the entire expense incurred in replacing the Gorham bridge.

Ithiel Town is said to have been more of a promoter than a builder.

There have been suggestions that the truss he patented was not his invention, but was already in use! At any rate, he realized he had a good thing and took care to advertise it by pamphlets as well as trips around the country. He even went to Europe to sell his ideas to foreigners. An able businessman, he sold rights to build his truss to many of our bridge builders. One of them was Sanford Granger, born in New Hampshire in 1784. He worked in that neighborhood until his death in 1882 at Bellows Falls, where he had built the Tucker toll bridge, one of a long list of structures large and small. A careful workman with high standards, many of his bridges are still in use.

A more shadowy figure among Town's licensees is one Fergusson, who enters the Vermont scene with the Clapp bridge in Montgomery. While there he employed the Jewett brothers and taught them the lore of his craft so they were able to build the rest of Montgomery's bridges, using the lattice type of truss. All over New England local carpenters were being converted to Town's invention. An engineering magazine states that as late as 1900 the Boston & Maine railroad had at least 100 lattice truss bridges in service. Almost all of these were built without the aid of engineers by skilled carpenters who had adopted bridge-building as a life work. How much credit is due to the type of truss and how much to the excellent craftsmanship of these men is beside the point. The fact remains that covered wooden bridges, properly designed and well maintained, have lasted at least as well as steel and concrete. Experience has shown that their removal by flood has been, as Captain Nemo puts it, an incident rather than an accident. They could be replaced, rebuilt, or salvaged, which is not often true of steel. They were easily and cheaply strengthened to carry new and greater loads, so their effective life was of amazing length. Perhaps there is a lesson in this for modern highway engineers, now that government priorities make steel so hard to get. Perhaps, too, it may prove wiser to repair the old bridges rather than build new. At least one Vermont town has faced the problem in the current

Fig. 89: INTERIOR OF TAFTSVILLE BRIDGE, WOODSTOCK
A mongrel Long truss with laminated arches added

year (1941) and is spending $4,000 to fix up their old bridge instead of $40,000 for a new one of steel and concrete.

Good as it is, Town's lattice truss is not the only wooden one that is available today. In 1830, Colonel Stephen H. Long of the U. S. Topographical Engineers patented the truss that bears his name and was granted patents on improvements in 1836 and 1839. It was planned as an

Fig. 90: BARNET VILLAGE BRIDGE, STEPHENS RIVER
A modified Long truss is used here

all-wood truss, although cast iron or steel has been used in connection with it. It never became popular, for some reason. Perhaps he was not as good a salesman as Ithiel Town. Many rural highway bridges which were built by local carpenters were hybrids of the Long and Burr types, like the Taftsville bridge in Woodstock (fig. 89). Because of the big X-braces in the panels of the truss it is often confused with Howe's invention. It takes an engineer to explain the difference! Barnet's village bridge (figs.

Fig. 91: BARNET VILLAGE BRIDGE FROM STEPHENS RIVER
The end wood of floor framing should be covered

90, 91) is constructed with a modification of the Long truss, and in this case there is no arch. The exceedingly vulnerable parts of its floor framing would be better protected if the upright boarding on the sides were covered with clapboards to guard the end wood of the floor beams from the spray of the waterfall.

The development of railroads brought new requirements for the bridge builders. At the same time it gave an impetus to the manufacture of iron that made it easier to procure quantities of iron rods and bolts which tended to replace wooden tension members and treenails just as cast iron replaced carefully shaped oak bearing blocks. Following the trend of the times, trusses were designed that were part wood, part iron. The first of these was invented by William Howe, a Massachusetts architect, who patented it in 1840. During that year he built a great railroad bridge at Springfield, Mass., Amasa Stone being associated with him. The following year Stone bought Howe's patent rights, formed a company, and built this type of bridge in many parts of the country. It was the basis of innumerable bridges built during the ensuing half century until displaced by all-steel bridges.

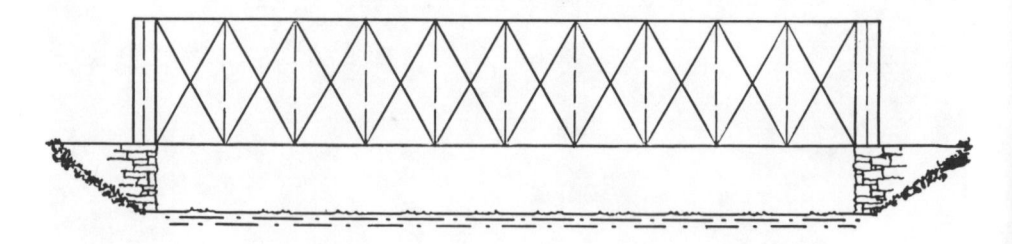

Fig. 92: DIAGRAM OF A HOWE TRUSS
Solid lines indicate wood, broken ones, iron

The Howe truss was the first to use iron as an essential material, not a mere convenience, and marks the transition between the old all-wood trusses and the modern all-steel ones. As the diagram (fig. 92) indicates, iron was employed for the vertical tension rods, but wood was retained for the upper and lower chords, the end posts and the diagonal braces or struts. In the larger trusses these struts form an "X" but many of the smaller ones used single diagonals sloping in towards the middle of the bridge. Our Vermont bridge-carpenters, if they used this truss, varied its details cheerfully, according to their individual preferences. Like other patent trusses that they copied, the result is either a variation or a mongrel, according to the observer's personal opinions. The two bridges across the Connecticut's upper reaches, mentioned in an earlier chapter, are the nearest to pure Howe trusses that can be found in Vermont. Engineer-de-

Fig. 93: LORD'S CREEK BRIDGE, IRASBURG
Small size and distinguished simplicity

signed and carpenter-built, the choice of the Howe truss with its generous use of wood indicates that the old-fashioned bridge is still considered a good investment.

Our bridge builders took understandable pride in their work. They were not content with good construction; they took what little opportunity they had to make their bridges good looking, and the portals were the only place where they could add that little extra touch of beauty that marks the master craftsman. Their approach to this part of the design was primarily functional; the basic idea was the protection of expensive framework from the weather. Nevertheless, the builder who really cared

Fig. 94: NORTHFIELD FALLS VILLAGE BRIDGE, DOG RIVER
A square-headed opening. Note the pilasters

about the appearance of his work might give this protection in a way that added real distinction to the front of the bridge. Some bridges, their openings sheltered by the bold projection of the gable, rose as straight up in front from bottom to roof as they did at the sides. Ohers had the gable supported on long sloping brackets, the arch overhanging the floor by a couple of feet. And there usually was a portal arch, originally at least. Perhaps the opening had an arched head because it just looked better that way. Perhaps there was a thought in the back of the bridge designer's head that a load of hay had a rounding top and by using the curve he

Fig. 95: BRIDGE OVER BLACK RIVER AT DOWNERS, WEATHERSFIELD
The gable end treated like that of a house

could let a big load of hay through and still keep the rain off the floor boards. Whatever the reason, there was generally an arch over the entrance, and a graceful one.

A few bridges were designed without the sloping end-struts that are generally used to make a more rigid connection between the roof and trusses. In this type a square-headed opening was almost inevitable. The builder of the Northfield Falls village bridge (fig. 94) evidently did not care for the severity of such a treatment, and by adding a few very simple mouldings gave the effect of pilasters, a dollar's worth of effect for every penny's worth of material. The station sign-board "ornament" is a more

Fig. 96: SCHOOLHOUSE BRIDGE IN LYNDON
Poised like a bird about to fly

recent addition. The railroad company found it expedient to abandon their stop at this tiny hamlet and demolished the station. The stationmaster had spent fifty years in it and his adjoining house and it is said he put the sign up on the bridge so he could feel more at home.

More rarely, the gable might be treated in the same manner as the end of a house, with a simple cornice resting on what architects call "returns" and with a narrow casing to outline the arch. This shows in the bridge at Downers in Weathersfield (fig. 95). The present ramshackle condition suggests a pronounced change of sentiment towards what was once considered a valuable piece of town property. No explanation has been

Fig. 97: VILLAGE BRIDGE ACROSS WATERBURY RIVER, STOWE
An admirable solution of the sidewalk problem

found for this unusually fine treatment—or its present neglect. The Schoolhouse bridge in Lyndon (fig. 96), being on the edge of a particularly neat little village is as well kept as it is designed. This is a happy solution of a problem in design. The builder wanted to protect his structure from the effect of weather, so he spread the eaves much wider than is usual, and also carried his gable out on tall, sloping brackets. To get a harmonious appearance with what might have been unpleasing features, he repeated the curve of the middle arch at the sides. The result is light and graceful, suggesting a bird poised to take wing. In less skillful hands the big roof on a small bridge might have looked like Grampa's hat on little Willy. The villagers have taken advantage of the spreading roof to add a sidewalk under its shelter, a much more pleasing disposition of this modern convenience than usual. It is perhaps the only bridge in the state

Fig. 98: LEVIS BRIDGE, WEST HILL BROOK, MONTGOMERY
Even white paint did not save this portal

to have the trusses boarded in on both sides. Lyndon is to be congratulated on cherishing a precious relic, a real asset to an attractive community. Not every village has as good an opportunity to add a sidewalk to its bridge.

In these days a separate footwalk is necessary for the safety of pedestrians and motorists alike. To be satisfactory, the addition should look as if it had always been there or it will arouse the wrath of conservatives and be dubbed "that wart of a sidewalk." Stowe has reached an admirable solution (fig. 97). Their utterly plain old bridge attracts and satisfies the eye because of its perfect proportions. When they added the sidewalk they set the roof at the same slant as that of the bridge, and adding vir-

Fig. 99: SECOND OTTER CREEK BRIDGE, BRANDON

tue to virtue, made its portal of just the right width and height to make an exceedingly subtle relationship to that of the bridge, a delicate refinement known to sophisticated designers.

An amazingly wide variety of portal designs were made from the simple elements of opening, gable and eaves. It is interesting that none of them were fancy, like those on some former bridges across the Delaware. Vermont carpenters preferred simplicity, yet they did like to make sightly entrances. It has been left to their successors to mar the good looks of many an old bridge. The weather-boarding has to be replaced in due time. It takes a certain amount of thought to cut the new boards to the

Fig. 100: INTERIOR, FAIRFAX VILLAGE BRIDGE

old arch-shape. Usually there are diagonal braces at the entrance, to which the boards are nailed and it is all too easy to follow that sloping line when sawing away the surplus material. Without the arch, the beauty of the portal may be seriously affected. It is true that some bridges never had arched openings. Some were deliberately designed with square heads. Others show that it is possible to make a passably goodlooking entrance with a horizontal upper line that slopes down at the corners to the upright sides. The sloping lines, however, should be made parallel to the slope of the gable if there is to be a harmonious result. This can be better understood by comparing the portals of Brandon's second bridge across Otter Creek (fig. 99), in which this has been done, with the Fairfax village

Fig. 101: HIGH BRIDGE IN WINTER; CLAY BROOK, WAITSFIELD

Photo by M. L. Joslin.

bridge (fig. 86). This has forty-five degree slants in the corners which make a most unpleasant contrast with the flatter angle of the gable. An arch would obviate this clash, especially if it could start higher. Looking at the illustration of the interior of the Fairfax bridge (fig. 100) it is plain this would be easy to do. There seems to be no good reason why the diagonal brace at the portal should not match those farther inside the bridge. It would be interesting to know if there was once an arch here.

Now the type of man who designs and builds bridges thinks differently from one who is only a member of a repair-gang. He *cares* about good looks. He builds to get as pleasing an appearance as possible without neglecting functional considerations. The repair man is chiefly inter-

Fig. 102: BROWN'S RIVER BRIDGE, WESTFORD

ested in getting the job done so he may go on to the next one. There is a good deal to say for each attitude. Luckily for the old bridges we have a goodly number of people, in and out of office, who really want to see the charm of the old work preserved. It is they who are responsible for the careful restoration of many an admirable feature of the bridges that are left. Undoubtedly many taxpayers with justifiable pride in their town properties will keep up their good work and continue to see to it that their investments are not only maintained in safety, but preserved from thoughtless repairs that are damaging to their appearance.

Unfortunately, trucks do more damage to bridge portals than age does. The road commissioner of Montgomery states that he has to replace the portals of their bridges about every year, and that the cause is careless driving rather than big loads. There seems little to choose between snipped-off corners and arched heads for safety from such injuries. The remedy may be a greater degree of cooperation on the part of citizens.

After all, the whole matter goes back to developing a more widespread interest in our old bridges and especially, a liking for the things about them that seemed important to their builders.

Perhaps it is a risky business to try to define these. It is certain that a man who works by hand in wood looks at his work from a very different angle from the one who merely nails on machine-cut lumber, rough from the saw. Disregarding those bridges that have evidently lost their decorative features through thoughtless replacements, we find plenty of material on which to base plausible opinions. Only about half of Vermont's remaining bridges are illustrated in this book, to avoid what seems repetitious, yet in that half there are many examples of bridge portals worth preservation. They are the only portion of a bridge where the builders could relieve functional severity with decoration. They utilized their opportunity. Only the simplest means were used; perhaps merely a couple of pieces of wood to suggest a pilaster. The very simplicity of the detail is an attribute of genius. To the casual observer it is trivial, the crude effort of a well meaning country carpenter. It may be so in some cases; but not in all, by any means. Unbiased critical examination of the work of some of our unschooled forebears often commends their good taste over that of some modern "registered architects." Repairs and replacements, then, should be done with care if the effect originally planned is to be preserved.

A surprisingly large number of persons are interested in covered wooden bridges. Of course, many are swayed by sentimental feelings, a nostalgia for what once was—or might have been. Others have deeper motives than sentiment. They are keenly alive to the fitness of the old bridges to the rural scene, or, with one hand on their pocket-books, are beginning to wonder if the costlier steel-and-concrete is not an extravagance on back roads and dead-end byways. And then there are those who honestly admire the handiwork of old times and wish to see it preserved in its original condition wherever practical. It is not always easy to reach an unbiased opinion of the meaning of "practical," either. There are those who have a fad for the modern just as some have a fad for the old-fashioned. Perhaps it is less a fad than a realization of the excellence of work produced by our forefathers in a less hurried age. Whatever their reasons for wanting the covered bridges retained, this constantly increasing number of taxpayers can make its desires effective through the orderly procedure of town meetings. In Vermont's functioning democracy "those who pay the piper call the tune."

REFERENCES

Connecticut River Valley in Southern Vermont and New Hampshire,
    by Lyman S. Hayes. Tuttle Company, Rutland, Vermont, 1929
    A collection of short articles giving useful history and anecdotes of the neighborhood covered by the title.

Covered Bridges in America,
    by Rosalie Wells. William Edwin Rudge, New York, 1931
    Illustrations of 135 bridges in 25 states.

Covered Bridges in Windham County, Vermont (pamphlet),
    Articles from Brattleboro Daily Reformer, 1937, edited by Victor Morse
    An exceedingly interesting series with much useful information.

Covered Bridges of California, The,
    by S. Griswold Morley. University of California, 1938
    A study of bridges old and new in a state that is still building them
    Lists 44, naming types of truss used, dimensions and dates.

Covered Bridges of New England,
    by Clara Wagemann. Tuttle Company, Rutland, Vermont, 1931
    Illustrated with etchings by George T. Plowman.

History of the Development of Wooden Bridges (pamphlet).
    by Robert Fletcher and J. P. Snow. Paper No. 1864, American Society of Civil Engineers, New York, 1934
    A masterly treatment of the subject, technical yet easily understood by laymen.

Iron Mining and Smelting in Bennington, Vermont,
    by John Spargo. Bennington Historical Museum, 1938

Letter, Theodore Burr to Reuben Field
    In Lancaster, Pennsylvania, Historical Papers, Volume XI

Sketch of the Civil Engineering of North America,
    by David Stevenson. John Weale, London, 1838

Vermont in Flood-time, (pamphlet),
    by Luther B. Johnson. Roy L. Johnson Company, Randolph, 1928
    Readable and informative; many half-tone illustrations.

INDEX

Abandoned Bridge, 21, 22, 24, *fig.* 8
Accuracy of work, 83, 86
Adams, Luther, 88
Age of covered railroad bridges, 107
Advertising posters, 56, 71, *figs.* 40, 41
Aiken, George D., 45
Albany, Black River bridge, 48, *fig.* 28
Albany, New York, 33, 34
Allen, Richard S., 20
Allen, Seth, 49
Altitude, highest, 40, *fig.* 24; lowest, 44, *fig.* 25
Anchor rods, 69, 70, *figs.* 41, 44, 45
Appreciation of early builders, 64
Arched portals, 37, 134, 140, 141, *figs.* 15, 18, 24, 26, 28, 32, 46, 49, 65, 90, 93, 95, 96
Arches, laminated, 31, 117, *figs.* 12, 78; hewn, 31, 116, 117, 125, *figs.* 12, 78, 88
Arch truss, tied, 60, *fig.* 38
Arlington bridge, 68, *fig.* 44

Babbitt brothers, 94, 95
Barnet Village bridge, 130. 131, *figs.* 90, 91
Barrels and Bridges, 37, 89
Barre railroad bridge, 105
Battenkill River bridge, 67, 68, *fig.* 44
Beaver Meadow Brook bridge, 80, 81, 123, *figs.* 57, 84
Bedell's bridge, 96, *fig.* 64
Belknap, Daniel. 88
Bellows Falls bridges, 25, 26, 28, 74, *fig.* 10
Belvidere bridge, *fig.* 1
Bennington bridge, 24, 33, 34, *figs.* 15, 16
Billings, Avery, 48
Billings bridge, 47, 48, *fig.* 27
Black Falls Brook bridge, 18, *fig.* 5
Black River bridges, 44, 46, 48, 49, 120, 121, *figs.* 26, 28, 82, 95
Black walnut timbers, 22
Blake, Frederick J., 27
Boston & Maine R.R. bridges, 128
Boyce, Deacon David E., 31, 76
Bracing, lateral, 65, 70, 117, 123, 124, *figs.* 51, 73, 78, 88
Bracketed portal, 77, *fig.* 53

Brandon bridges, 102, 103, 139, *figs.* 67, 99
Brattleboro bridge, 52, 53, 109, 110, *fig.* 31
Brattleboro-Hinsdale toll bridge, 109, 110
Breckinridge James, 33
Bridge Census, 20, 21
Bridge materials, 53, 54, 82
Bridges, salvaged, 24, 37
Broad Brook bridge, 121, *fig.* 83
Brookfield, Floating bridge, 87, 89, *fig.* 60
Brown County, Indiana, 22
Brown's River bridges, 23, 142, *figs.* 9, 102
Building a bridge, 83, 84, 85
Burned bridge, 61, 95, 114
Burr-arch truss, 30, 31, 96, 114, 116, 117, 119, *figs.* 12, 76, 78, 79
Burr, Theodore, 114, 121, 122

California bridges, 22
Camber, 84
Cambridge bridges, 61, 116, 119, *figs.* 77, 78, 80, 81
Captain Cook's daughter, 122
Census, bridge, 20, 21
Charlotte bridges, 44, 45, 60, 61, 79, *figs.* 25, 38, 55
Charter conditions tolls, 92
Chenoweth, Lemuel, 81
Chiselville bridge, 39, 40, *fig.* 20
Chord, 110, 111, 122, 123
Clapboarding 71, *fig.* 47
Clapp bridge, Montgomery, 128
Clay Brook bridge, 141, *fig.* 101
Clyde River bridges, 60, *fig.* 36
Cobb (Governor's) Brook bridge, 52, *fig.* 30
Colonel Hale's bridge, 25, painting of, 27
Columbia bridge, 95, *fig.* 63
Combination trusses, 125, *fig.* 88
Compression, 110
Comstock bridge, 79, *fig.* 56
Concrete facing, 79, 80, 81, *figs.* 56, 57
Concrete supports, 77, 81, *figs.* 52, 57
Connecticut River bridges, 21, 25, 26, 28, 74, 92, 94, 95, 96, 97, 99, 100, 102, *figs.* 10, 61, 62, 63, 64, 65

Construction, 83, 84, 85
Contest for longevity, 53, 54
Converted bridges, 67
Cornish-Windsor bridge, 97, fig. 65
Cornwall bridge, 69, 70, fig. 46
Costs of bridges, 50, 94, 129
Covered Bridge, The, 13
Covered wooden railroad bridges, 105, 106, figs. 69, 70
Creamery bridge, 53, fig. 31
Crossing on the ice, 87, 100

Danville, Greenbank Hollow bridge, 67, fig. 43
Definition of a truss, 110
Destruction by fire, 61, 95, 114
Deutsches Museum, 27
Development of covered bridge, 65
Dog River bridge, 134, fig. 94
Doubled trusses, 34, fig. 16
Double-lane bridges, 28, 29, 115, 116, figs. 11, 12, 77, 78
Downer bridge, 135, 136, fig. 95
Dry walls, 76, 77, 78, figs. 53, 54, 57

Early bridge-builders, 64
East Charleston bridges, 60, fig. 36
East Charlotte, Upper bridge, 79, fig. 55
East Creek bridges, 57, 59, 48, 104, figs. 35, 68
East Montpelier bridge, 108, fig. 71
Effect of railroads on toll-income, 97
Eldridge, "Wib", 48
Enosburg bridges, 19, 80, 81, 123, figs. 6, 57, 84
Evading payment of tolls, 99, 100

Factor of safety, 109
Fairfax bridges, 23, 123, 140, 141, figs. 9, 86, 100
Falling-off of toll income, 97
Falsework, 39, 83, 84, 85, 87
Fergusson, bridge builder, 128
Fire, destruction by, 61, 95, 114
First Branch bridge, South Royalton, 21, 22, fig. 8
First toll-freed bridge, 102
Fishing bridge, St. Albans Bay, 56, 57, fig. 34
Floating bridge, 87, fig. 60
Flood damage, 23, 37, 73, 117
Flood-years, 23, 32, 36
Ford, Henry, 22, 87
Freeing of tolls, 92

Freeing toll bridges, 100
Fuller Bridge, Montgomery, 18, fig. 5

Gable, overhanging, 134, figs. 7, 26, 28, 41, 45, 49, 54, 65, 74, 77, 90, 93, 94, 95
Gable treatment, 135, 136, fig. 95
Garfield bridge, 40, fig. 23
Georgia Plains, Pierce's Mill bridge, 62, 67, fig. 41
German bridges, 22
Geyer, 27
Gorham bridge, 20, 37, 126, 127, fig. 7
Governor's (Cobb) Brook bridge, 52, fig. 30
Granger, Sanford, 27, 52, 128
Greatest number of bridges in county, 51
Greenbank Hollow bridge, 67, fig. 43
Green River bridges, 40, 43, 54, 55, 56, figs. 23, 32, 33
Guildhall-Lancaster bridge, 92, fig. 61
Guilford bridge, 54, 55, figs. 32, 33

Hale's bridge, Colonel, 25, painting of, 27
Hale, Enoch, 26
Halpin bridge, 40, fig. 21
Hammond bridge, 36, 37, 127, fig. 17
Hardwick railroad bridge, 105, 106, fig. 69
Harnois bridge, 71, fig. 48
Hartland bridge, 68, 70, fig. 45
Haunted bridges, 49
Haverhill-Newbury (Bedell's) bridge, 96, fig. 64
Havre-de-Grace bridge, 86
Head bridge, 71, fig. 48
Hectorville Bridge, 14, fig. 2
Henry bridge, 33, 34, 35, figs. 15, 16
Hewn arches, 31, fig. 12
High Bridge, Waitsfield, 141, fig. 101
High bridges, 39, 40, 41, 42, 43, figs. 20, 21, 22, 23, 24
High water over floor, 117
Highgate Falls toll bridge, 15, 16, fig. 3
Highwaymen, 47, 48
Historical Society, Lancaster, 121
Holland bridge, 50, 51, fig. 29
Holton, Erastus M., 52
Hopkins bridge, 19, fig. 6
Howe truss, 95, 96, 132, 133, figs. 63, 92
Howe, William, 132
Hubbell's Falls bridge, 117, fig. 79
Hybrid trusses, 130, figs. 89, 90, 91
Hyde Park, Garfield bridge, fig. 43

Indiana bridges, 21, 22
Inside boarding, 38, 71, 138, *figs.* 42, 48, 96
Investment-value, 22
Irasburg bridges, 44, 46, 133, *figs.* 26, 93
Iron bridge, legendary, 50, 51
Iron mines, 34
Iron, pure, endurance, 73
Iron rods, 69, 73, 111, 112, 131

Jefferson bridge, 61
Jewett Brothers, 80, 128

Kapell Brücke, 22
Kelton, Lovel, 109
Kingpost truss, 110, 111, *fig.* 72
Kingsley, architect, 109, 110
Kirby road, bridge, 112, *fig.* 74
Kissing Bridge, 18, 19, 20, *fig.* 7

Lafayette at Windsor bridge, 97
Lake Champlain bridges, 44, 57, *figs.* 25, 34
Lake Shore bridge, 44, 45, 60, *figs.* 25, 38
Laminated arches, 31, 73, 76, *figs.* 12, 51
Lamoille County, 51
Lamoille River bridges, 6, 61, 112, 115, 116, *figs.* 1, 73, 77, 78
Lamson, Caleb B., 87
Lancaster-Guildhall toll bridge, 92, 93, *fig.* 61
Lancaster Historical Society, 121
Lancaster-Lunenburg toll bridge, 94, *fig.* 62
Lattice truss, 28, 31, 34, 83, 122, 123, 124, 125, 126, 127, 128, *figs.* 10, 16, 31, 33, 47, 48, 49, 51, 56, 57, 58, 68, 84, 85, 88, 100
Leaning bridges, 34, 35, 36, 69, 70, 123, 125, *figs.* 15, 46, 86
Lemington-Columbia bridge, 95, *fig.* 63
Lengths of bridges, 27, 87, 89, 97
Letter from Theodore Burr, 121
Levis bridge, 138, 142, *fig.* 98
Lewis bridge, 52, *fig.* 30
Lewis Creek bridges, 76, 77, 79, *figs.* 52, 55
Loads on bridges, 109
Long, Col. Stephen H., 129
Longevity contest, 53, 54
Longey bridge, 71, *fig.* 48
Long's truss, 129, 131, *figs.* 89, 90, 91
Long-time collection of tolls, 97
Lord's Creek bridge, 133, *fig.* 93
Lotteries, 91
Lowe, Leslie, 50
Lowest bridge, 44, *fig.* 25

Lull's Brook bridge, 68, 70, *fig.* 45
Lunenburg-Lancaster bridge, 94, *fig.* 62
Luzern, Kapell Brücke, 22
Lyndon bridges, 112, *fig.* 74

Mad River bridge, 31, 32, *figs.* 13, 14
Mansfield, Mount, 23, 118, 119, *figs.* 9, 80
Marshfield private bridge, 101, 103, *fig.* 66
Martin's Mill bridge, 68, 70, *fig.* 45
Mead bridge, 125, 126, 127, *figs.* 87, 88
Middlebury bridges, 28, 29, 31, 40, 41, 75, *figs.* 11, 12, 21, 50, 51
Mill Brook bridge, Fairfax, 125, *fig.* 86
Mill Brook bridge, West Windsor, 60, 61, *fig.* 37
Miller Brook bridge, 112, *fig.* 75
Missisquoi River bridges, 16, 70, 106, *figs.* 3, 47, 70
Models, 81, 82
Modern practise, 23, 63, 96, *figs.* 62, 63
Modified designs of trusses, 118
Mongrel trusses, 119
Monteith, James, toll-gatherer, 98, 99
Montgomery bridges, 14, 18, 42, 71, 80, 138, *frontis.* and *figs.* 2, 5, 22, 48, 56, 98
Montpelier & Wells River R. R. bridge, 105
Morgan bridge, 40, 44, *fig.* 24
Mortgage, 27
Moseley bridge, 37, *fig.* 18
Moseleys, father and son, 37
Most popular truss, 123
Mount Mansfield, 23, 118, 119, *figs.* 9, 80
Mount Orne bridge, 94, 95, *fig.* 62
Muddy Branch bridge, 40, 41, *fig.* 21
Murders in bridges, 48
Museum-pieces, 22, 85
McCall's Ferry Bridge, 121

Neckar bridge, new, 22
Newbury toll bridge, 96, *fig.* 64
Newest bridge, Vermont's, 37, 38, *fig.* 18
Newfane Village bridge, 77, *fig.* 53
New Hampshire bridges, 21, 25, 28, 92, 94, 95, 96, 97, 99, 100, 102, *figs.* 10, 61, 62, 63, 64, 65
New Hampshire Grants, 33
North Blenheim bridge, 85
North Branch bridge, 121, *fig.* 82
North Ferrisburg, Lewis Creek bridge, 77, *fig.* 52
Northfield, Rocky Brook, 37, 38, *fig.* 18

Northfield Falls bridge, 134, 135, fig. 94
North Troy bridge, 70, fig. 47
Nourse, Asa, 37

Oak timbers, 22; treenails, 83, 123, fig. 58
Oatman, Daniel, 39
Ohio bridges, 21
Oldest bridge, Switzerland, 22; Vermont, 28, 29, 32, 33
Old-fashioned truss, 38, 120, figs. 19, 82, 83
Old '76 bridge, 48, 104, fig. 68
Ompompanoosuc River bridge, 78, fig. 54
Open bridges, 64, 67, fig. 42
Otter Creek bridge, 69, 70, 139, figs. 46, 99
Otter Creek bridges, 20, 29, 30, 31, 34, 37, 69, 74, 75, 103, 125, 126, 127, 139, 140, figs. 7 11, 12, 17, 46, 50, 51, 67, 87, 88, 99
Overhang (gable), 134, figs. 7, 26, 28, 41, 45, 49, 54, 65, 74, 77, 90, 93, 94, 95
Owen, Abraham, 126, 127

Palmer on weather-protection, 65, 66
Papermill bridge, 28, 31, 117, figs. 11, 12
Passumpsic River bridges, fig. 74
Pennsylvania bridges, 21
Pierce's Mill bridge, 67, fig. 41
Pilasters, 134, 135, 143, figs. 15, 35, 94
Pine Brook bridge, 110, fig. 72
Pins, wooden, 83, 123, fig. 58
Pioneer Junction railroad bridge, 105
Pittsford bridges, 20, 36, 37, 126, figs. 7, 17
Pittsford Mills bridge, 87
Pleasant Valley bridge, 119, figs. 80, 81
Pointing, 79, figs. 55, 56
Popular truss, 123
Portals, 37, 133, 134, 135, 136, 137, 139, 142, 143, figs. 86, 94, 95, 96, 97, 99, see Arched Portals, Bracketed Portals, Slant-cornered Portals, Square-headed Portals.
Posse comitatus, 33
Post Mills bridge, 78, fig. 54
Powers, Charles, 86
Powers, Daniel C., 126
Powers' Folly, 85
Powers, Nicholas M., 59, 81, 82, 85, 87, 126
Preventive masonwork, 80, fig. 57
Private bridges, 101, 103, figs. 66, 67
Proctor bridges, 20, 37, 126, 127, figs. 7, 87, 88
Pulpmill bridge, 28, 31, 117, figs. 11, 12

Queenpost truss, 111, 112, figs. 73, 74

Railroad bridges, 74, 105, 106, figs. 69, 70
Railroad bridge, long-lived, 74
Ralph, Orlando, 89
Ramp Creek bridge, 22
Randolph bridges, 38, 39, fig. 19
Repairing masonry, 79, 80, figs. 55, 56, 57
Restored bridges, 39, 48, 104, 129, fig. 19
Restoring a "condemned" bridge, 104, 129
Rhine bridge, old, 22
Road equipment, 21
Roaring Branch bridge, 39, 40, fig. 20
Robberies in bridges, 47, 48
Royalton bridges, 22, 121, figs. 8, 83
Running the bridge, 28, 99, 100
Rutland bridges, 48, 59, 104, figs. 35, 68

Safford bridge, 119, figs. 80, 81
Saint Albans Bay bridge, 56, 57, fig. 34
St. Johnsbury & Lake Champlain R. R. bridges, 105, 106
Salisbury bridge, 69, 70, fig. 46
Salvage, 24, 37
Saxton's River village bridge, 72, fig. 49
Schoolhouse bridge, 136, 137, fig. 96
Scott bridge, 49
Second bridge, Brandon, 139, 140, fig. 99
Secondary chords, 122, 123, fig. 84
Sheriff Ten Eyck, 33
Shingle Mill bridge, 80, 122, figs. 57, 84
Sidewalk addition, 32, 33, 130, 136, 137, 138 figs. 14, 90, 96, 97
Simple truss, 110
Size of bridges, 44
Slant-cornered portals, 140, 141, figs. 5, 8, 11, 34, 37, 48, 54, 80, 86, 99, 100
South Royalton bridge, 21, 22, fig. 8
Specifications, 82
Spruce, strength of, 54, 82
Square-headed portals, 134, 135, 140, figs. 7, 17, 35, 41, 57, 61, 77, 83, 94, 97
Station sign-board, 134, 135, fig. 94
Steel tubing, 23
Stein-Säckingen bridge, 22
Stephens River bridge, 130, 131, figs. 90, 91
Stevenson, David, 83
Stiffness of trusses, 124
Stock companies, 92
Stone, Amasa, 132
Stone-work, 76, 78
Storehouse bridges, 21, 56, figs. 8, 33
Stowe bridges, 112, 137, 138, figs. 75, 97
Strength of bridges, 50, 109

Stringers, 24, 27, 73
Strongest bridge, Vermont's 35, 36
Strut, 110, 112
Sunderland, 38, 40, *fig.* 20
Swanton railroad bridge, 106, *fig.* 70

Taft Brook bridge, 124, *fig.* 85
Taftsville bridge, 129, 130, *fig.* 89
Taking down trusses, 124
Tasker, James, 97
Tension, 110
Test of bridge's strength, 109
Thalhausen bridge, 22
Thetford, Post Mills Bridge, 78, *fig.* 54
Three-mile Bridge, 31, 75, *figs.* 50, 51
Tied arch truss, 60, *fig.* 38
Tie-rod, iron, 111
Toll-book notations, 97
Toll bridges, 15, 16, 25, 26, 28, 92, 94, 95, 96, 97, 99, 100, 102, *figs.* 3, 10, 61, 62, 63, 64, 65
Toll-gate, 99, *fig.* 65
Toll rates, 92
Towing upstream, 37
Town, Ithiel, 122, 127, 128, 129
Town road equipment, 21, 56, *figs.* 8, 33
Townshend, 49
Town truss, *see* Lattice truss
Traffic figures, toll-bridge, 97
Treenails, 83, 123, *fig.* 58
Trout River bridges, 14, 19, 71, 79, 80, *frontispiece*, *figs.* 2, 6, 48, 56
Truck damage, 138, 142, *fig.* 98
Truss, definition, 110
Trusses, varieties: See list, page 10 and Burr, Howe, Kingpost, Lattice, Long, Old-fashioned, Queenpost, Simple, Tied-arch, Town, Warren
Tucker, Nathaniel, 27, 28
Tucker toll bridge, 26, 28, *fig.* 10
Tunbridge, 17; bridge over First Branch White River, *fig.* 4

Twin bridges, East Charleston, 59, *fig.* 36 Rutland, 58, *fig.* 35
Tying to banks, 69, *figs.* 41, 45

Uses of bridges, odd 21, 46, 47

Vermont bridges, 21

Waitsfield bridges, 31, 32, 110, *figs.* 13, 14, 72
Walloomsac River bridge, 33, 34, 35, *figs.* 15, 16
Waltham Turnpike Company, 29, 32
Warning signs, 40, 47, *fig.* 39
Warp ng of trusses, 123
Warren truss, 112, *fig.* 75
Waterford, New York, bridge, 31, 114, 121
Weather-boarding, 66, 139
West Arlington bridge, 68, *fig.* 44
West Dover bridge, 64, 65, *fig.* 42
West Dummerston bridge, 87, 88, *fig.* 59
West Hill Brook bridge, 40, 42, *fig.* 22 and frontispiece
West River bridges, 49, 50, 51, 77, 87, *figs.* 29, 53, 59
West Windsor bridge, 60, *fig.* 37
Westford bridge, 142, *fig.* 102
Westminster Lewis bridge, 52, *fig.* 30
Weybridge bridge, 29, 30, 31, *figs.* 11, 12
Whetstone Brook bridge, 53, *fig.* 31
White River bridges, 17, 21, 22, 38, 39, *figs.* 4, 8, 19
Wind-bracing, 64, 68, 70, *figs.* 42, 47
Wind damage, 68, 70, *fig.* 46
Windham County, 51
Windsor toll bridge, 97, 98, *fig.* 65
Winooski River bridges, 101, 103, 105, 108, *figs.* 66, 71
Wolcott bridge, 112, *fig.* 73
Wolf-hunt crosses Windsor bridge, 97
Wooden pins, 83, 123, *fig.* 58
Woodstock bridge, 129, 130, *fig.* 89
Woods used, 53, 54, 82